Cash flow statements

A commentary on FRS 1 (revised 1996)

Cash flow statements

A commentary on FRS 1 (revised 1996)

By Jyoti Ghosh BSc, FCA
of Coopers & Lybrand, Chartered Accountants

London, November 1996

This book aims to provide general guidance only and does not purport to deal with all possible questions and issues that may arise in any given situation. Should the reader encounter particular problems he is advised to seek professional advice, which Coopers & Lybrand would be pleased to provide.

No responsibility for loss occasioned to any person acting or refraining from action as a result of any material in this publication can be accepted by the author or publisher.

Appendix 1 is reproduced with the permission of the Accounting Standards Board.

Coopers & Lybrand is authorised by the Institute of Chartered Accountants in England and Wales to carry on investment business.

ISBN 1 85355 753 6

Contents

Contents

Chapter 1

Executive Summary

Introduction

1.1 On 31 October 1996, the Accounting Standards Board (ASB) published a revised version of its Financial Reporting Standard on cash flow statements. The revision – FRS 1 (Revised 1996) – replaces the original FRS 1 issued in September 1991.

1.2 The revision draws on the practical experience of FRS 1 in use and reflects the responses to FRED 10 issued in December 1995. Its provisions apply to accounting periods ending on or after 23 March 1997, but earlier adoption is encouraged.

1.3 Under the original FRS 1, the cash flow statement reported movements in cash and cash equivalents (that is, investments with maturities of up to three months). Many were critical about the definition of cash equivalents and its limited use in assessing the true liquidity position of an entity. As a result, FRED 10 proposed to drop cash equivalents and reform cash flow reporting to bring it more into line with business practice. The changes proposed by FRED 10 were widely welcomed and the revised standard is based on those proposals with minor refinements.

1.4 Under the revised standard, only movements in actual cash will be shown as cash flows. The heading 'investment activities' has been dropped and all treasury activities will now be reported together under a new heading, 'management of liquid resources'. This heading will include cash flows relating to treasury investments (previously included in investing activities) and former cash equivalents. Cash flows relating to treasury activities can now be viewed as a whole. As a result, the statement is now a genuine cash flow statement – the first in the world. A new reconciliation links the cash movements in a period to changes in net debt (borrowings less cash and liquid resources). The format of the statement has also been radically redesigned. The changes introduced should enable entities to communicate more effectively information about their liquidity, solvency and financial adaptability.

Principal changes from the old FRS 1

1.5 The principal changes from the old FRS 1 may be summarised in the paragraphs that follow.

1.6 A cash flow statement should focus on identifying the cash effects of transactions with parties that are external to the reporting entity and their impact on its cash position. Only those transactions that involve a *cash flow* should be reported in the cash flow statement. For this purpose cash is defined as cash in hand and deposits repayable on demand with any qualifying financial institution, less overdrafts from any qualifying institution repayable on demand.

1.7 The revised standard radically changes the current format of the cash flow statement. Cash flows that under the original FRS 1 were included under 'investing activities' will now be analysed into two new headings: 'capital expenditure and financial investment' and 'acquisitions and disposals'. As stated above, the revision also introduces a new heading 'management of liquid resources'. Equity dividends paid by the reporting entity will now be reported separately after 'acquisitions and disposals'.

1.8 The revised format adopts the following eight headings and cash flows should be reported under the headings in the order in which they are set out below:

- Operating activities.
- Returns on investments and servicing of finance.
- Taxation.
- Capital expenditure and financial investment.
- Acquisitions and disposals.
- Equity dividends paid.
- Management of liquid resources.
- Financing.

1.9 It is now permitted to show the individual categories of cash inflows and outflows under the above standard headings in a note so as to avoid clutter on the face of the cash flow statement. In addition, cash inflows and outflows may now be shown *net* in certain restricted circumstances, for example if they relate to a constantly renewed short-term facility or a commercial paper programme. The revised order and headings represent a major improvement and would fit in more easily with the way managements describe their businesses.

1.10 Net cash flows from operating activities would include dividends received from equity-accounted entities provided their results are included as part of operating profit. Operating cash flows should also include cash flows relating to provisions for operating items, whether or not the provision was included in operating profit. For example, redundancy payments included as part of the provision for costs of a fundamental reorganisation or a business closure reported outside operating profit will be included in operating cash flows.

1.11 Companies may choose whether to present the existing reconciliation of operating profit to operating cash flow in the notes or as introduction to the cash flow statement. If the latter approach is adopted, the note should be separately identified and clearly labelled to maintain the distinction that it is not part of the primary cash flow statement. The reconciliation should also show separately the difference between dividends received and results taken into account for equity accounted entities.

1.12 Cash flows under 'returns on investments and servicing of finance' will no longer include equity dividends paid by the reporting entity. These are to be shown separately under a new heading (see below).

1.13 No changes are proposed to the current reporting of taxation cash flows, except that subsidiary undertakings should include cash received and paid in respect of group relief under this heading.

1.14 Cash flows under 'capital expenditure and financial investment' relate to the acquisition or disposal of (a) any fixed asset (including investments), except a trade, business or entity that should be classified under 'acquisitions and disposals' (see below) and (b) any current asset investments not included in liquid resources. If no cash flows relating to financial investment fall to be included under this heading the caption may be reduced to 'capital expenditure'.

1.15 Cash flows under 'acquisitions and disposals' relate to the acquisition or disposal of any trade, business or entity that is an associate, joint venture or subsidiary undertaking. The revised standard requires separate disclosure of any balances of cash and overdraft acquired or transferred on acquisition or disposal, which are currently netted off against consideration cash flows.

1.16 Equity dividends paid by the reporting entity should be shown separately to recognise the fact that such payments, unlike interest, are not contractual in nature.

1.17 As stated above, 'management of liquid resources' is a new heading that arises as a result of the abolition of cash equivalents and the need to distinguish cash flows relating to treasury activities from other investing activities. Liquid resources are defined as any current asset investments held as readily disposable stores of value. Therefore, any current asset investment can be a liquid resource provided it can be readily converted into cash at or close to its carrying value or traded in an active market, without disrupting or curtailing the entity's business. Liquid resources are to be identified by each reporting entity according to its policy (which must be disclosed), but can only include current asset investments. This new heading will improve the information provided on treasury activities that was not previously available to the extent that the instruments dealt in fell within the definition of cash equivalents.

1.18 Cash flows reported under 'financing' are the same as those reported under the original FRS 1, except that issue costs on non-equity shares and debt instruments are moved to 'returns on investments and servicing of finance' to achieve consistency with FRS 4.

1.19 A new note reconciling the movement of cash in the period with the movement in net debt should now be included, either at the end of the cash flow statement or in a note. Net debt is defined to include capital instruments that are liabilities as defined in FRS 4, together with obligations under finance leases less cash and liquid resources. The reconciliation is not part of the cash flow statement and, if presented at the foot of the cash flow statement, it should be clearly labelled and kept separate. The reconciliation would provide information about changes in liquidity on a broader basis than that provided solely by the movement in cash balances as reported in the cash flow statement. In addition, a note should be included analysing the change in net debt with the related items in the opening and closing balance sheets. This new note effectively combines the existing notes relating to (a) the movement in cash and cash equivalents and (b) the items shown under the financing section of the cash flow statement, and links them to the related items in the opening and closing balance sheets for the period.

1.20 There is now a requirement to disclose any cash flows that are exceptional because of their size or incidence, irrespective of whether or not they relate to items that are reported as exceptional in the profit and loss account. Sufficient disclosure of the nature of the exceptional item and the related cash flows should also be given in a note to the cash flow statement so that users may gain an understanding of how these transactions have affected the reporting entity's cash flows.

1.21 Intra-group cash flows between members of a group located in different countries may be translated at the actual rate, if known, in order to ensure that they cancel out on consolidation. If the rate used to translate intra-group cash flows is not the actual rate, any exchange difference arising should be included in the effect of exchange rate movements shown as part of the reconciliation to net debt.

1.22 There should be disclosure of any restrictions on the ability of the group to transfer funds from one part of the group to another, provided access is severely restricted by external factors such as exchange control regulations.

Scope

1.23 The revision of FRS 1 is not intended to change its scope in a major way, but there are some changes. The revised standard extends the exemption from preparing a cash flow statement for wholly-owned subsidiaries to cover subsidiaries where 90 per cent or more of the voting rights are controlled within the group provided the consolidated financial statements in which the subsidiary undertaking is included are publicly available. It is no longer necessary for those consolidated financial statements to include an FRS 1 cash flow statement or for the parent undertaking to be an EU company. There are also specific exemptions for pension funds and open-ended investment funds meeting certain conditions. The existing exemption for building societies has been extended for a further two years to give the ASB time to develop consensus and seek the necessary changes to the building society legislation.

1.24 Except for the above exemptions, the provisions of the FRS apply across all industry groups since cash flow is relevant to all businesses. This means that banks, insurance companies and other financial institutions have to present cash flow information. Because of the special nature of their businesses, FRS 1 requires slightly different formats for banks and insurance companies. A bank need not include a section on the management of liquid resources nor the reconciliation of cash flows to the movement in net debt.

Insurance companies should include a section on 'portfolio investments' rather than cash flows relating to the 'management of liquid resources'. An analysis of the movement in portfolio investments less financing rather than an analysis of net debt would also be required. Examples of possible formats for a bank and an insurance group are included in the standard.

Effective date

1.25 The revised standard supersedes FRS 1 issued in September 1991 and is mandatory for accounting periods ending on or after 23 March 1997 but earlier adoption is encouraged. It is likely that a number of companies with December 1996 year ends will take the opportunity to adopt the standard for those accounts.

Chapter 2

Introduction

2.1   The success, growth and survival of every reporting entity depends on its ability to generate or otherwise obtain cash. Cash flow is a concept that everyone understands and with which they can identify. Reported profit is important to users of financial statements, but so too is the cash flow generating potential of an enterprise. What enables an entity to survive is the tangible resource of cash not profit, which is merely one indicator of financial performance. Thus, owners look for dividends, suppliers and lenders expect payments and repayments, employees receive wages for their services, and the tax authorities are legally entitled to tax revenues due.

2.2   Yet the provision of cash flow information by UK companies, as part of their external reporting function, is a relatively new phenomenon. Until the issue of FRS 1, 'Cash flow statements', in September 1991, which came into effect for accounting periods ending on or after 23 March 1992, there was no requirement in the UK to prepare a cash flow statement. Instead, UK companies provided a funds statement under SSAP 10, 'Statements of source and application of funds'.

Limitations of SSAP 10

2.3   SSAP 10 was issued in 1975 and required that audited financial statements should include a statement of source and application of funds. However, there was little formal prescription concerning the structure and content of the funds statement. Consequently, in practice, a wide variety of different presentations were found, some of which were very informative while others were less so. This flexibility in funds statement reporting practices had the effect of reducing comparability between statements and, therefore, their usefulness.

2.4   Perhaps the principal shortcoming of SSAP 10 was that the statement simply provided an analysis of the sources and application of funds (however defined) in terms of the movements in assets, liabilities and capital that had taken place during the year, rather than in terms of how the various activities of the business had either generated or absorbed funds. The result was that the funds statement merely listed the changes in balance sheet totals, thereby giving little, if any, additional information and so explained little about a company's ability to meet obligations or to pay dividends or about its need for external financing.

2.5 Numerous interpretations of the word 'funds' were used in practice. Narrowly defined, funds were taken to mean net liquid funds, the only term defined in SSAP 10, whilst at the other extreme funds included all the financial resources of the company. In between these two extremes fell definitions such as working capital and net borrowings. The effect was that there was very little comparability between the funds statements of different companies.

Development of cash flow reporting under FRS 1

2.6 The advent of cash flow reporting was a direct consequence of the shortcomings of the funds flow reporting practices adopted under SSAP 10. These shortcomings were further exposed by the much publicised failures of some reputable listed companies during the late 1980s that had been widely regarded as profitable. In order to address these shortcomings, and also to keep pace with the significant international developments that had already taken place in cash flow reporting particularly in the USA and Canada, the ASC, prior to its demise, published ED 54, 'Cash flow statements', in July 1990.

2.7 ED 54 proposed that a cash flow statement should be required in place of the funds flow statement under SSAP 10. The exposure draft proposed that cash flows should be classified according to the operating, investing and financing activities of the business. Although the exposure draft provoked much comment, it was generally felt that the quality of the information provided by a cash flow statement was superior to that produced by a funds flow statement. The ASB took over this project as one of its top priorities and published FRS 1 in September 1991.

2.8 Whilst retaining the general thrust of ED 54, FRS 1 made significant changes to the structure of the cash flow statement proposed in ED 54 and introduced two additional standard headings, 'returns on investments and servicing of finance' and 'taxation'. It also exempted a larger number of reporting entities from preparing cash flow statements.

FRS 1 in practice

2.9 The ASB's first financial reporting standard has been in operation for about five years. It was generally well received and many listed companies saw advantages in FRS 1 and adopted the statement early. However, as preparers and users became accustomed to the standard, a number of practical matters, some more fundamental than others, arose.

2.10 The original standard required that the cash flow statement should include all the reporting entity's inflows and outflows of cash and cash equivalents. Although the concept of cash was readily understood, it was the definition of cash equivalents that caused the greatest difficulty in practice. The standard classed deposits with more than three months to maturity when acquired as investments, not cash equivalents. Critics argued that their exclusion from cash equivalents failed to capture their substance. Company treasurers normally take a longer view of their cash management function and do not draw a distinction between investments and cash in the way envisaged by the old FRS 1, or if they do they draw a different distinction. As a result, they believed that the three month rule was of little or no relevance to their treasury management operations and of limited use in assessing the true liquidity position of the company. Critics also argued that a narrow definition of cash equivalents was not consistent with the objective of FRS 1, which asserted that the purpose of the cash flow statement was to assist users of the financial statements in their assessment of the reporting entity's liquidity, viability and financial adaptability.

2.11 In practice, companies chose to deal with the shortcomings of the definition of cash equivalents in a variety of ways. Generally companies have tended to follow the strict definition of cash and cash equivalents in preparing their cash flow statements, but have also adapted the format and/or given additional information that reflects the way in which they manage their cash flows. For example, some companies have chosen voluntarily to disclose the movements of net cash/net debt, which they regard as more useful information than the movements in cash and cash equivalents, because it gives a better indication of the liquidity of the business. Others have taken a more radical approach by including short-term investment movements in financing on the grounds that they manage their borrowings and investments as an integrated treasury operation, making investments when rates are good and drawing down on borrowings when rates are low. These companies consider it misleading to show such investments as part of investing activities.

2.12 The ASB was aware of the concerns expressed above. Indeed when FRS 1 was first issued, the ASB indicated that it would review the standard after its first two years of operation. It kept its promise by calling for comments in March 1994 on how the standard could be improved. On 7 December 1995, after a long period of deliberation, the ASB issued FRED 10, 'Revision of FRS 1 Cash flow statements', which proposed significant changes to FRS 1.

Revision of FRS 1

2.13 The ASB worked hard to find a suitable alternative definition of cash equivalents, but found it impossible to reach a consensus. According to the ASB, preferred maturity periods for cash equivalents varied from as short as one month to as long as a year. Some suggested measuring the maturity of short-term investments from the balance sheet date (residual maturity) in place of the standard's measure of original maturity. In the end, the ASB went down a completely different route and proposed to overhaul significantly the way companies report their cash flows.

2.14 FRED 10 proposed to drop cash equivalents and to use only cash (cash in hand and at bank, less overdrafts) as the basis of the cash flows reported in the cash flow statement. A new format for the statement was proposed. Dividends paid and capital expenditure would be shown differently, in a way that would highlight free cash flows. The movements in former cash equivalents, which often formed part of a company's treasury activities, were proposed to be included under a new heading that deals with the management of liquid resources. In addition, FRED 10 proposed to split the 'investing activities' into two: 'capital expenditure' and 'acquisitions and disposals'. The proposals also firmly linked the cash flow statement with the profit and loss account and the balance sheet by introducing a reconciliation of cash flows to the movement in net debt as well as to operating profit.

2.15 The proposals in FRED 10 were novel and represented what is arguably the world's first pure cash flow statement. It picked up many of the suggestions that were made in response to the ASB's invitation to comment on FRS 1. It was a major improvement on the current version of the standard. The notion of 'cash equivalents' always was arbitrary and so it seemed sensible to move to a narrower measure of simply cash and to a broader measure of net debt. Both are measures that businesses use and understand.

2.16 It is, therefore, not surprising that the proposals in FRED 10 received a favourable response from all quarters. The revised standard, which was issued on 31 October 1996 and which is effective for accounting periods ending on or after 23 March 1997, is therefore closely based on FRED 10. Reference in this chapter to FRS 1 should be read as reference to the revised standard.

2.17 One possible drawback is that the revised FRS 1 moves the UK away from international practice. Both the international standard, IAS 7, and the US standard, SFAS 95, involve reporting changes in 'cash and cash equivalents' and allocate the cash flows into three headings. So a UK change that abandons cash equivalents and moves from five headings to eight hardly sounds like harmonisation. It isn't, but in this particular case, the UK is right to experiment with the new approach and, if successful, the IASC and other countries might consider it.

Chapter 3

Objectives and scope of FRS 1

Objectives

3.1 The principal objective of FRS 1 is to require reporting entities falling within its scope to:

- Report their cash generation and cash absorption for a period by highlighting the significant components of cash flow in a way that facilitates comparison of the cash flow performances of different businesses.

- Provide information that assists in the assessment of their liquidity, solvency and financial adaptability.
[FRS 1 para 1].

3.2 The above objective is consistent with the draft 'Statement of principles for financial reporting' being developed by the ASB. Chapter 1 of the exposure draft dealing with 'the objective of financial statements' makes it clear that a cash flow statement provides an additional perspective on the performance of an enterprise by indicating the amounts and principal sources of its cash inflows and outflows. This information is useful in assessing the implications for future cash flows of the enterprise's performance and is particularly relevant to an assessment of financial adaptability.

3.3 The form of cash flow reporting required under FRS 1 provides useful information on liquidity, solvency and financial adaptability that is additional to that provided by the profit and loss account and balance sheet. A combination of profitability and liquidity data enables users of financial statements to view both sides of the same coin when assessing corporate viability over time (business survival depends on both profits from operations and sound cash management). Reporting historical cash flows also helps management to discharge its stewardship function by showing an enterprise's past cash flows, solvency and liquidity performance. Although historical cash flow is not necessarily a good indicator of future cash flows, it may nevertheless help users to review the accuracy of their previous predictions and, therefore, act as a base for assessing future cash flow performance and liquidity.

3.4 The standard also sets out how cash flow information should be presented and how extensive it should be. A standard format results in uniform presentation of cash flow information and makes such information much more comparable among companies. This comparability should, as with the original FRS 1, make the information useful to investors, creditors and other users of financial statements.

Scope

3.5 There is no statutory requirement for companies to prepare a cash flow statement. However, FRS 1 requires all reporting entities that prepare financial statements intended to give a true and fair view of their financial position and profit or loss (or income and expenditure) to include a cash flow statement as a *primary* statement within their financial statements, unless specifically exempted. [FRS 1 paras 4, 5].

Available exemptions

3.6 The following entities are exempt from preparing a cash flow statement.

Subsidiary undertakings

3.7 A subsidiary undertaking, 90 per cent or more of whose voting rights are controlled within a group, is exempt from producing a cash flow statement, provided the consolidated financial statements in which the subsidiary undertaking is included are publicly available. [FRS 1 para 5(a)]. It should be noted that the original standard only exempted wholly-owned subsidiaries of EU parent companies from preparing a cash flow statement provided certain other conditions were satisfied. The revised standard extends the exemption to cover 90 per cent or more owned subsidiaries of any parent undertaking and also substantially relaxes the other conditions, such that the only condition is that consolidated financial statements in which the 90 per cent or more owned subsidiary undertaking is included are publicly available. Unlike the original standard, there is no requirement for the parent undertaking to prepare and make publicly available a consolidated cash flow statement that includes the cash flows of the subsidiary undertaking. This exemption is, therefore, similar to the 90 per cent or more exemption included in FRS 8, 'Related party disclosures' (see chapter 35).

3.8   Clearly, the extensions will allow a much wider range of subsidiary undertakings to claim the exemption than hitherto. In particular, all 90 per cent or more owned UK subsidiaries of parent companies incorporated outside the EU will be able to take the exemption from preparing a cash flow statement provided the parent's consolidated financial statements in which the subsidiary is included are publicly available. However, not all countries have a requirement to make financial statements available to the public. Publicly available normally means disclosure in a registry or by publication in a register or gazette. Laws requiring disclosure to shareholders alone are not laws requiring public disclosure. It would, therefore, appear that UK subsidiaries of say, a US parent that is not an SEC registrant, would not be able to claim the exemption, because there is no requirement in the US for such a private company to publish or otherwise make available its financial statements to the public.

Mutual life assurance companies

3.9   Mutual life assurance societies that are owned by policy holders and friendly societies that carry on mutual life assurance business are exempt from producing a cash flow statement. [FRS 1 para 5(b)].

Pension schemes

3.10 The SORP, 'Financial reports of pension schemes', does not require pension schemes to produce a cash flow statement. This is because information about the cash flows of the scheme is normally provided by the fund account and net asset statement. Although the fund account adopts an accruals basis of accounting rather than a strict cash flow basis, re-presenting the information in the format of a cash flow statement would generally not provide any significant additional information for the readers of pension scheme financial statements. The original FRS 1 did not specifically exempt pension schemes from its scope, but the revised standard grants exemption for pension schemes from preparing a cash flow statement, which is consistent with the SORP.

Open-ended investment funds

3.11 The standard exempts open-ended investment funds from producing a cash flow statement provided certain conditions are satisfied. For this purpose, the standard defines an investment fund by using three of the four conditions for qualifying as an investment company as set out in section 266(2) of the Act. [FRS 1 para 2]. The fourth condition, which prohibits capital profits from being distributed, is intentionally left out of the standard's definition so as to allow unauthorised unit trust type vehicles (often used for unquoted or venture capital investments) and certain investment entities whose trust deeds or articles do not prohibit distribution of capital profits to claim the exemption from preparing a cash flow statement.

3.12 Clearly, the exemption is broad and means that a wide range of authorised and unauthorised investment vehicles will not have to prepare cash flow statements. However, the exemption is conditional on meeting all of the following criteria:

- Substantially all of the entity's investments are highly liquid.
- Substantially all of the entity's investments are carried at market value.
- The entity provides a statement of changes in net assets.

[FRS 1 para 5(d)].

Most investment vehicles should have little difficulty in meeting the above conditions.

Building societies

3.13 Building societies, as defined by the Building Societies Act 1986, are currently required by section 72(1)(c) of that Act to produce a statement of source and application of funds in a prescribed format. The original standard exempted building societies from preparing a cash flow statement on the grounds that a cash flow statement, in addition to the statutorily prescribed statement, would result in the duplication of much of the information that could not be justified on cost-benefit grounds. The ASB believes that the exemption for building societies should be ended because of the similarity of their operations with banks, which are not given any exemption from producing cash flow statements. However, as the proposal depends on changes in building society legislation and related aspects of financial reporting for banks and building societies, the revised standard extends the exemption for building societies for two years from the effective date of its introduction. [FRS 1 para 5(e)].

Small companies and groups

3.14 Small (but not medium-sized) companies entitled to file abbreviated financial statements with the Registrar under section 246 of the Act need not prepare a cash flow statement. [FRS 1 para 5(f)]. Generally, a company qualifies as small if it meets the relevant conditions and the size criteria specified in the Act (see further chapter 36). A small company is not actually required to file abbreviated financial statements, but merely has to be entitled to do so in order to claim the exemption from preparing a cash flow statement. However, the exemption is not available where the small company is a public company, a banking company, an insurance company, an authorised person under the Financial Services Act 1986, or a member of a group containing one or more of the above mentioned entities.

3.15 The draft FRSSE prepared by the CCAB Working Party and submitted to the ASB for consideration does not contain a requirement for a smaller entity to prepare a cash flow statement. However, it is likely that the scope of the exemption will be re-examined when the report is finally considered by the ASB. In the meantime, small companies are encouraged to produce a cash flow statement as part of their financial statements if it would provide useful information to users and the benefits of doing so outweigh the cost of providing the information. [FRS 1 para 54].

3.16 Where a small company is also the parent company of a small group and the parent company claims the exemption under section 248 from preparing consolidated financial statements, a consolidated cash flow statement need not be prepared. Although this would appear to be obvious, the exemption is not specifically mentioned in FRS 1 as it only makes reference in paragraph 5(f) of FRS 1 to the exemptions for *small companies when filing accounts with the Registrar.* Nevertheless, it will have the effect of applying in practice. This is because if a parent company of a small group can claim the exemption from having to prepare consolidated financial statements, then it is certain that the parent company and each of its subsidiary undertakings will qualify as small companies in their own right and will individually be exempt from preparing a cash flow statement. Consequently, where a small parent claims the section 248 exemption from preparing consolidated financial statements, it will not have to include a consolidated cash flow statement or its own cash flow statement when preparing its individual financial statements.

3.17 Similarly, a consolidated cash flow statement is not required, for the reasons stated above, where the small group voluntarily prepares consolidated financial statements, although it may make sense to include a consolidated cash flow statement in this situation.

Medium-sized companies and groups

3.18 Medium-sized companies are not exempt from producing cash flow statements irrespective of whether or not they choose to file abbreviated financial statements with the Registrar.

3.19 For medium-sized groups, however, the position is not so clear cut. Generally, where a medium-sized group is entitled to claim the section 248 exemption from having to prepare consolidated financial statements and does so, a consolidated cash flow statement need not be prepared. But where a medium-sized group voluntarily chooses to prepare consolidated financial statements, it will have to produce a consolidated cash flow statement.

3.20 A particular problem faces the parent company of a medium-sized group where the parent company itself meets the small size criteria, but nevertheless is deemed to be a medium-sized company under section 246(5) of the Act. Where such a group claims the exemption from producing consolidated financial statements, the question arises as to whether the parent company can dispense with the need to produce a cash flow statement as part of its individual financial statements. The standard does not specifically exempt such a parent from producing a cash flow statement as part of its individual financial statements, because it does not fall to be treated as a small company under section 246(5) of the Act. Therefore, a small parent of a medium-sized group will have to prepare a cash flow statement as part of its individual financial statements where consolidated financial statements are not prepared. Furthermore, its 90 per cent or more owned subsidiary undertakings, which are unlikely to meet the small-size criteria, will have to include a cash flow statement as part of their individual financial statements. This is for two reasons. First they are unable to claim the small company exemption in their own right. Secondly, there is no exemption available to the subsidiary undertakings, because the parent does not produce consolidated financial statements that are publicly available.

Small unincorporated entities

3.21 Entities that are unincorporated, but would satisfy the criteria for small company exemptions had they been incorporated under the Act are exempt from preparing a cash flow statement. [FRS 1 para 5(g)]. They are, nevertheless, encouraged to prepare one if they consider it appropriate on cost-benefit grounds.

Other entities

3.22 Except for the above exemptions, the provisions of the FRS apply across all industry groups since cash flow is relevant to all businesses. This means that banks, insurance companies and other financial institutions have to present cash flow information. Because of the special nature of their businesses, FRS 1 requires slightly different formats for banks and insurance companies. Appendix I to the standard provides illustrations of amended layouts for cash flow statements for a bank and an insurance group.

Chapter 4

Preparation of cash flow statements

4.1   It is consistent with the objective stated in paragraph 3.1 above that a cash flow statement should focus on identifying the cash effects of transactions with parties that are external to the reporting entity and their impact on its cash position. Only those transactions that involve a *cash flow* should be reported in the cash flow statement. [FRS 1 para 6]. *Cash flow*, not surprisingly, is defined as an increase or decrease in an amount of cash. [FRS 1 para 2].

Definition of cash

4.2   As the cash flow statement only reflects movements in cash, the definition of cash is central to its proper preparation. The standard does not define cash as used in common parlance, but extends the definition to include overdrafts that are repayable on demand. Overdrafts are included in the definition because they are generally viewed as negative cash balances and effectively repayable on demand. Thus cash includes:

- Cash in hand, and also deposits, including those denominated in foreign currencies, *repayable on demand* with any bank or other qualifying financial institutions.

- Overdrafts from any bank or qualifying financial institutions repayable on demand.
[FRS 1 para 2].

For this purpose, a qualifying financial institution is an entity that as part of its business receives deposits or other repayable funds and grants credits for its own account. [FRS 1 para 2].

4.3   One impact of the definition of cash is that monies transferred between deposits that qualify as cash do not result in cash inflows and outflows, but are merely movements within the overall cash balance. For instance, a transfer from a deposit account to reduce the company's overdraft would not be reflected in cash flows as it is an intra cash movement. However, all charges and credits on accounts qualifying as cash, such as bank interest, bank fees, deposits or withdrawals other than movements wholly within them, represent cash inflows and outflows of the reporting entity.

Meaning of 'repayable on demand'

4.4 In order to qualify as cash, deposits must be *'repayable on demand'*, which they are if they meet one of the following criteria:

- They can be withdrawn at any time or demanded without notice and without penalty.

- A period of notice of no more than 24 hours or one working day has been agreed.

[FRS 1 para 2].

Without notice implies that the instrument would be readily convertible into known amounts of cash on demand, that is, not subject to any time restriction. Therefore, monies deposited in a bank account for an unspecified period, but which can only be withdrawn by giving notice of more than 24 hours or one working day would not fall to be treated as cash under the definition. However, such funds can always be withdrawn by paying a penalty. In some situations, this penalty payment may not be significant enough to cause any appreciable change in the capital amount withdrawn. Nevertheless, the standard makes it clear that cash is repayable on demand if it is in practice available within 24 hours *without penalty*. Therefore, repayable on demand implies both withdrawal without penalty and without notice, or if a notice period has been agreed it must not exceed 24 hours or one working day.

Definition of liquid resources

4.5 As can be seen from the above, the definition of cash is sufficiently narrow to exclude investments, however liquid or near maturity. Nevertheless, companies normally use a range of such investments like term deposits, gilts, money market instruments, listed equity securities, Euronotes, not for their investment potential, but for managing their overall cash or net debt position. If the focus of the cash flow statement is to report movements in pure cash, the question arises as to where in the cash flow statement movements in such investments which do not qualify as cash, but which are nevertheless used increasingly in cash management and treasury operations, should be reported.

4.6 The revised standard creates a separate heading 'management of liquid resources' within the cash flow statement for reporting the cash flows arising on such liquid investments. This heading differentiates investments that are effectively used in managing the entity's net debt or net funds position from those that are held for their investment potential. However, to qualify as a liquid resource, the investment must be held as a readily disposable store of value. To be held as a readily disposable store of value, the investment must be held as a current asset investment. Fixed asset investments, therefore, do not qualify, because by definition these are held for use on a continuing basis and so are not readily disposable. For this purpose, a readily disposable investment is one that is not only disposable by the entity without curtailing or disrupting its business, but also satisfies either of the following criteria:

- It is readily convertible into known amounts of cash at or close to its carrying amount.

- It is traded in an active market.
[FRS 1 para 2].

4.7 The first criterion is particularly relevant for classifying investments in short-term deposits. Although a measure of liquidity, or a maturity period, is not specifically mentioned in the definition, the standard explains that the criterion that the deposit should be readily converted into cash at or near its carrying amount would tend to exclude any that are more than one year from maturity on acquisition. [FRS 1 para 52]. A period of one year would also be consistent with the investment's classification in the balance sheet as a current asset investment, a condition that is necessary for the investment to qualify as a liquid resource.

4.8 Liquid resources meeting the first condition are likely to encompass investments held with qualifying financial institutions that are short-dated and on which there are very little price fluctuation between the time the deposit was made and its ultimate conversion into cash. Therefore, it does not matter whether a term-deposit can be withdrawn by giving notice of more than 24 hours or whether the deposit can be withdrawn prior to its maturity by payment of a penalty, provided the penalty is not significant to cause any appreciable change in capital value. It does not also matter whether the maturity period is of a short duration (say three months) or medium duration (say six months to a year). As long as the deposit is readily convertible into a known amount of cash at or near its carrying amount and there are no restrictions as to the investor's ability to dispose of the investment without curtailing the business, it will qualify as a liquid resource. Deposits intended to be held for a long term, say between one and two years, are unlikely to qualify, even though they may be used by the entity in managing its overall cash or debt position. This is because, according to the definition, they are not sufficiently liquid. Therefore, any movements in them would fall to be reported under capital expenditure and financial investments.

4.9 The second condition allows current asset investments such as government securities, equity and debt instruments in other entities and derivative instruments to be treated as liquid resources, provided they are traded in an active market. Where an active market exists, the inference is that the instruments are easily exchangeable into known amount of cash and, hence, will represent readily disposable stores of value. Therefore, unlisted investments held as current assets are unlikely to qualify as liquid resources.

4.10 As explained in paragraph 2.14, the scrapping of the former 'cash equivalents' and the introduction of 'liquid resources' represents a neat solution to the major drawback in the former standard. No regard normally needs be paid to when investments will mature or whether they are convertible into known amounts of cash without notice (that is, effectively available immediately at face value) or whether they are subject to any capital value risk. Provided they represent readily disposable stores of value, and meet either of the conditions set out in paragraph 4.6, a wide range of current asset investments will qualify as liquid resources. The emphasis now is on a wider measure of liquidity rather than the type of the investment. The standard does not *require* all readily disposable investments to be classified as liquid resources. An entity can *choose* which of its current asset investments will be treated as liquid resources. However, it would need to explain its policy and any changes to its policy (see further para 6.40).

Treatment of borrowings

4.11 Borrowings, whether short or long-term, do not qualify as liquid resources, although bank overdrafts repayable on demand are included in cash (see para 4.2). It follows that, except for bank overdrafts, cash flows arising from all forms of borrowings, including commercial paper, should be included within the financing section of the cash flow statement. This is a change from the original standard under which short-term bank advances repayable within three months from the date of advance were included within cash equivalents.

Chapter 5

Format of cash flow statements

Introduction

5.1   To achieve the objective of providing information to help investors, creditors and others in making assessments about the liquidity, viability and financial adaptability of an entity, the standard requires cash flows to be classified under the following standard headings:

- Operating activities.
- Returns on investments and servicing of finance.
- Taxation.
- Capital expenditure and financial investments.
- Acquisitions and disposals.
- Equity dividends paid.
- Management of liquid resources.
- Financing.

5.2   The cash flows for each of the headings should be listed in the order set out above. However, the last two headings may be combined under a single heading relating to the management of liquid resources and financing provided the cash flows relating to each are shown separately and separate subtotals are given. [FRS 1 para 7]. Some companies that manage their liquid investments and borrowings as an integrated treasury operation, making investments when rates are good and drawing down on borrowings when rates are low, and matching investments with borrowings, may find this ability to combine the two headings particularly useful.

5.3   Striking a subtotal after any of the above headings is neither required or prohibited. Therefore, it is possible to strike a subtotal, for instance, after capital expenditure and before acquisitions and disposals. Indeed, some entities may consider it appropriate to highlight this figure as it indicates a measure of 'free cash flow' that their businesses have generated and over which they have discretionary spending ability. Although this measure does not necessarily distinguish between discretionary capital expenditure for expansion from that incurred for routine replacement and presumes that acquisitions and, more importantly, disposals are discretionary, which may not be the case, it may nevertheless be useful. Others may find it preferable to strike a subtotal after equity dividends paid as indicated in the illustrative examples in the standard. The ability to strike a subtotal at any level will, therefore, enable entities to highlight cash flows that they consider appropriate to their particular circumstances.

5.4 There is also a degree of flexibility allowed in the reporting of the individual elements of cash inflows or outflows that make up each of the standard headings. Although these individual cash inflows or outflows should not be netted against each other, except in certain circumstances as explained in paragraph 5.9 below, they could either be reported gross on the face of the cash flow statement under the appropriate standard headings or shown in the notes. This means that it is acceptable to include merely the (net) totals for each of the above headings on the face of the cash flow statement, which would obviously avoid clutter on the face of the cash flow statement and possibly make it easier to understand.

Classification of cash flows

5.5 A cash flow statement must classify cash receipts and cash payments under each of the eight standard headings. The classification of cash flows into reasonably distinct groups provides useful analysis about the relative importance of each of these groups and the inter-relationship between them. It should also provide useful information for comparison purposes across reporting entities.

5.6 The standard provides specific guidance for classifying cash flows. It sets out each individual element of cash inflows and outflows that should be included under a particular standard heading. Enterprises are required to disclose separately, where material, the individual categories of cash flows within each standard headings, either in the cash flow statement or in a note [FRS 1 para 8]. The way in which elements of cash flow are attributed to each standard heading is considered from paragraphs 6.1 below.

5.7 There are other elements of cash flows, not considered in the standard headings, that may cause classification difficulties. Clearly, it is not possible for the standard to provide an exhaustive list of all types of different cash flows. Consequently, the standard stipulates that where a cash flow is not specified in the categories set out in the standard headings, it should be shown under the most appropriate standard heading in accordance with the transaction's substance. [FRS 1 para 10]. Since the transaction's substance also determines the way in which it is normally reported in the profit and loss account and the balance sheet, it follows that there should be consistency of treatment in the cash flow statement and in the other primary statements. This requirement for consistency, which was not included in the original standard, would eliminate subjectivity in classifying cash flows not identified as specific items under the standard headings. [FRS 1 para 57]. Therefore, following this general principle, cash outflows relating to development expenditure that are capitalised in the balance sheet would fall to be shown under capital expenditure in the cash flow statement. Similarly, where the expenditure is written off as part of operating profit in the profit and loss account, the cash outflows would fall to be included in operating cash flows. Another example is the receipt of a government grant. To the extent that the grant is made as a contribution towards fixed assets, the substance argument would require the cash receipt to be shown under capital expenditure in the cash flow statement, irrespective of whether it is reported in the balance sheet as a deduction from the cost of the specific asset or included as deferred income and amortised over the expected useful economic life of the asset. Similarly grants given as a contribution towards revenue expenditure should be included in operating cash flows to match their treatment in the profit and loss account.

5.8 There is one situation where the general rule of classifying cash flows according to the transaction's substance is not considered appropriate. This applies to interest paid that is capitalised, for instance, as part of the construction cost of an asset in the balance sheet. Following the general rule would require reporting the interest paid under capital expenditure in the cash flow statement. However, all interest paid is specifically required to be shown under 'returns on investments and servicing of finance' heading, regardless of whether or not it is capitalised in the balance sheet. [FRS 1 para 10].

Gross or net cash flows

5.9 Generally cash inflows and outflows under each of the standard headings should be reported gross, whether on the face of the cash flow statement or in a note to it. However, there are some exceptions. These are as follows:

■ The reporting of gross cash flows does not apply to operating activities where the indirect method is followed (see para 6.5).

- Cash inflows and outflows relating to the management of liquid resources or financing may be netted against each other provided the inflows and outflows meet either of the following conditions:

  - They relate in substance to a single financing transaction which satisfies all the four conditions set out in paragraph 35 of FRS 4.

  - They are due to short maturities and high turnover occurring from rollover or reissue (for example, a commercial paper programme or short-term deposits).

[FRS 1 para 9].

5.10 The ability to net cash inflows and outflows relating to the management of liquid resources or financing is a significant improvement over the strict requirements of the original standard. Many large industrial and commercial companies raise funds by issuing commercial paper in the form of unsecured promissory notes with fixed maturity between seven and 364 days. Normally these are issued at a discount to the face value and provide a cheaper source of finance than other means of borrowing. A commercial paper programme may involve issues and redemptions throughout the financial year and often these are backed up by committed bank facilities. Prior to the revision of the standard, all movements in cash flows (issues and redemptions) during the year should strictly have been reported gross in the financing section of the cash flow statement. In practice, these were often shown net. Many argued that it is not only desirable, but necessary for a better understanding of the financing cash flows to report these potentially large inflows and outflows, for what may in substance be a continuing source of finance, on a net basis.

5.11 The ASB accepted the above argument and the revised standard accordingly introduces a requirement for net reporting for the limited class of items that fulfils either of the two conditions above. The FRS 4 conditions are discussed in detail in chapter 18. An example of a company that has reported the net change in the obligation under a commercial paper programme is given in Table 1 below.

Table 1 – Bass PLC – Annual Report – 30 September 1995

GROUP CASH FLOW STATEMENT (extract)

For the year ended 30 September 1995	Note	1995 52 weeks £m	1995 52 weeks £m	1994 53 weeks £m	1994 53 weeks £m
Financing					
Net movement of commercial paper		(60)		181	
Other new borrowings		135		99	
Other borrowings repaid		(69)		(115)	
		6		165	
Ordinary share capital issued		27		23	
Financing			33		188

5.12   Similarly, short-term funds that are continuously rolled over by successive deposits and withdrawals will fall to be reported net under the second condition. A question arises as to whether netting is permissible in circumstances where withdrawals from short-term deposits and payments into short-term deposits are effected with different parties. The standard is silent on this point, but in practice, treasurers often withdraw funds from one party and place them on deposits with another party to increase the overall returns on those funds. Therefore, as long as the short-term deposit is constantly renewed or rolled over, whether with the same party or with a different party, it is acceptable to report the cash inflows and outflows on a net basis.

5.13   The ability to report net cash flows in relation to rollover and reissue transactions effectively brings the UK standard in line with IAS 7 and the US FAS 95. The alternative of showing the gross amounts for raising and repaying money under a commercial paper programme or constantly renewable short-term deposits would not add very much to users' understanding of a company's treasury activities.

Additional classification

5.14   The individual items of cash inflows and outflows set out under each of the standard headings in FRS 1, other than operating activities, should not be regarded as depicting a rigid set of classification rules. The analysis under each heading merely refers to those items that would normally fall to be included under that heading and, hence, prescribe a minimum acceptable level of disaggregation of cash flow information. The individual items may be further sub-divided or new items added, if appropriate, to give a full description of the activities of the business or to provide segmental information. [FRS 1 para 8]. Indeed, the standard encourages entities to disclose additional information relevant to their particular circumstances. [FRS 1 para 56]. For example, repayments of amounts borrowed may be sub-divided further to show payments made on the redemption of debentures and other repayments of long-term borrowings. Another example would be to divide the cash flows from operating activities into those relating to continuing activities and those relating to discontinued operations (see further para 10.4).

5.15 Whatever level of detail is disclosed, it must be sufficient and relevant so that the user is able to understand the relationship between the entity's different activities and the way in which they generate and expend cash. On the other hand, too much information can cloud or obscure key issues. The problem is one of striking a balance between what the entity needs to report and how much explanation is required by the users. There is no definitive solution to this problem, because so much depends on the reporting entity's circumstances and the specific needs and expertise of the users.

Departure from the standard presentation

5.16 Prior to its revision, the original standard acknowledged that there might be circumstances where the standard presentation would not give a fair representation of the reporting entity's activities. In such rare situations, the standard called for the exercise of informed judgement to devise an appropriate alternative treatment. In practice, however, companies have rarely, if ever, departed from the standard presentation. As a result, the need to devise an appropriate alternative presentation has been deleted from the revised standard. Therefore, entities can add new items within each of the standard headings, but can no longer use a different heading, or depart from the format headings, unless there are grounds for invoking the true and fair override.

Chapter 6

Classification of cash flows by standard headings

Cash flow from operating activities

6.1   Cash flows from operating activities generally include the cash effects of transactions and other events relating to the operating or trading activities of the enterprise. The net cash flow from operating activities, therefore, represents the movements in cash resulting from the operations shown in the profit and loss account in arriving at operating profit. In addition, cash flows relating to any provision in respect of operating items, whether or not the provision was included in operating profit, should also be included as part of operating cash flows. For example, cash flows in respect of redundancy payments provided as part of the cost of a fundamental reorganisation or closure of operations that is reported outside operating profit in accordance with FRS 3 'Reporting financial performance', will fall to be included in operating cash flows (see para 6.48). Similarly, operating cash flows will also include cash flows in respect of provision for integration costs following an acquisition. [FRS 1 para 11].

6.2   Operating cash flows should also include dividends received from equity-accounted entities where their results are included as part of operating profit. [FRS 1 para 11]. Prior to the standard's revision, dividends received from equity-accounted entities were always shown under the heading 'returns on investments and servicing of finance'. The amendment is consistent with the recent trend of reporting the operating results of equity accounted entities as part of the investing group's operating results and with the treatment proposed by FRED 11 'Associates and joint ventures'. However, many companies continue to disclose their share of results from equity accounted entities after operating profit. Consequently, these companies should continue to show dividends received from their associates under 'returns on investments and servicing of finance' until such time as FRED 11's proposals are developed into an FRS.

6.3   Operating cash flows may be reported on the gross or net basis (also known as the direct method and the indirect method respectively). [FRS 1 para 7]. Under the direct method, the major classes of gross operating cash receipts (for example, cash collected from customers) and gross operating cash payments (for example, cash paid to suppliers and employees) are reported on the face of the cash flow statement under operating activities. An example of the direct method of presentation for net operating cash flow is illustrated in Table 2.

Table 2 – Marks and Spencer p.l.c. – Annual Report and Financial Statements – 31 March 1996

Consolidated cash flow statement (extract)

FOR THE YEAR ENDED 31 MARCH 1996

	Notes	1996 £m	1995 £m
OPERATING ACTIVITIES			
Received from customers		**7,046.0**	*6,665.0*
Payments to suppliers		**(4,741.9)**	*(4,426.3)*
Payments to and on behalf of employees		**(928.4)**	*(782.8)*
Other payments		**(566.9)**	*(547.1)*
Net cash inflow from operating activities	24	**808.8**	*908.8*

Notes to the financial statements (extract)

24 RECONCILIATION OF OPERATING PROFIT TO NET CASH INFLOW FROM OPERATING ACTIVITIES

	THE GROUP	
	1996 £m	1995 £m
Operating profit	**940.2**	*896.5*
Depreciation	**160.4**	*150.7*
Increase in stocks	**(45.8)**	*(22.4)*
Increase in customer balances	**(190.2)**	*(144.5)*
Increase in other debtors	**(109.6)**	*(22.7)*
Increase in creditors	**53.8**	*51.2*
Net cash inflow from operating activities	**808.8**	*908.8*

Operating profit has increased by £43.7m whereas the net cash inflow from operating activities of £808.8m is £100.0m lower than last year. This reflects the £90.0m payment in respect of the pension scheme deficit (see note 10A) together with an increase of £45.7m in the movement of customer balances within Financial Services.

6.4   The ASB allows, but does not require, reporting entities to provide information on gross operating cash flows. [FRS 1 para 58]. However, the standard makes it mandatory to provide a reconciliation between operating profit and net cash flow from operating activities as discussed in paragraph 6.6 below, *even where the direct method is adopted* as indicated in Table 2 above. For this reason and because of the additional burden of producing gross cash flow information where these figures are not directly available from the accounting system, the direct method has not been very popular with companies despite its theoretical soundness.

6.5 Under the indirect method, the same operating cash flows as under the direct method are reported except that the net figure is produced by adjusting operating profit for non-cash items (such as depreciation) and changes in working capital (such as accruals and prepayments) and bringing in cash flows relating to any provision in respect of operating items, whether or not the provision was included in operating profit. However, in keeping with the objective that a cash flow statement should only include items of pure cash flows, the standard requires that under the indirect method the cash flow statement should start with the net cash flow from operating activities.

Reconciliation of operating profit to net cash flow from operating activities

6.6 The reconciliation of operating profit to net cash flow from operating activities is not part of the cash flow statement. However, companies may choose whether to present the reconciliation as a supplementary note to the cash flow statement, or adjoining the cash flow statement. This latter approach, absent from the original standard, has been introduced to counter criticism that the positioning of this reconciliation far away from the cash flow statement itself is not very helpful. However, if the latter approach is adopted, the reconciliation statement should be separately identified and clearly labelled to maintain the distinction that it is not part of the primary cash flow statement. [FRS 1 para 12]. This is because the reconciling items are not themselves cash flows and to report them as part of the cash flow statement itself would be inappropriate. However, we do not regard it ideal for the reconciliation to introduce the cash flow statement as illustrated in example 1 in Appendix 1 to the standard. The reconciliation statement in that example is presented immediately under the general heading 'cash flow statement' and appears to be part of the cash flow statement itself, which is clearly not the intention. It is also confusing to have two headings for cash flow statement on the same page. A way of dealing with this is to entitle the page something along the lines 'information on cash flows'. The term 'cash flow statement' could then be used to describe the statement itself. A way of avoiding the problem is to position the reconciliation either under the cash flow statement or in a note immediately following it.

6.7   The reconciliation should disclose separately the movements in stock, debtors and creditors related to operating activities and other differences (for example, depreciation including profit or loss on sale of fixed assets included within operating profit, provisions, etc) between cash flow and operating results (see worked example at the end of the chapter). In addition, where the share of associated company's results is reported as part of operating results, the reconciliation should show separately the difference between dividends received and results taken into account for equity accounted entities. [FRS 1 para 12]. Cash flows from investments accounted under the equity method are considered further from paragraph 8.4.

6.8   For the reconciliation to be properly carried out, it will be necessary to analyse the movements in opening and closing debtors and creditors in order to eliminate those movements that relate to items reported in the standard headings other than operating activities. For example, a company may purchase a fixed asset prior to the year end on credit. In this situation, the closing creditor balance would need to be adjusted to eliminate the amount owing for the fixed asset purchase before working out the balance sheet movements for operating creditors. It follows that movements in working capital included in the reconciliation would not be the same as the difference between the opening and the closing balance sheet amounts. Indeed, under FRS 1 this is rarely the case except in very simple situations. This is because the balance sheet movements in stock, debtors, and creditors may be affected by such items as acquisitions and disposals of subsidiaries during the year (see para 8.10), exchange differences on working capital of foreign subsidiaries (see example para 9.18) and other non-cash adjustments for opening and closing accruals of non-operating items.

6.9   A question arises as to whether the eliminated items within each balance sheet movement of working capital need to be reported separately so that the overall movement between the opening and closing balance sheet amounts is readily understandable. For example, a company could identify the total balance sheet movement in creditors and then separately itemise the operating element and the other movements. The standard is silent on this point and in practice, this is rarely done; only the operating movement is reported. An example where a company has provided a detailed reconciliation between the movements in operating working capital reported in the reconciliation of operating profit to operating cash flows and the corresponding balance sheet movements is given in Table 3. Whether shareholders, investors and other users of financial statements are really interested in this degree of detail is debatable as it serves no more than a mere arithmetical check. The contrary view is that if a reconciliation is presented, it will be beneficial only if the amounts are capable of being individually traced back to the amounts shown under the equivalent captions in the balance sheet.

Table 3 – BTR plc – Report and Accounts – 31 December 1995

NOTES (extract)

		Consolidated	
£ millions		**1995**	1994

26 CASH FLOW STATEMENT (extract)

a) Reconciliation of operating profit before interest and tax to net cash inflow from operating activities

	1995	1994
Profit before interest and tax	**1,673**	1,546
Depreciation	**413**	389
Reorganisation provisions in respect of acquisitions	**64**	
Investment income	**(32)**	(35)
Net movement in working capital (trade and other):		
Inventories	**(134)**	(60)
Debtors	**(91)**	(103)
Creditors	**25**	22
Movement in provisions for liabilities and charges	**(126)**	(66)
Profits on disposal of subsidiaries and investments	**(170)**	(99)
Profit on disposal of properties	**(1)**	
	1,621	1,594

b) Balance sheet movement reconciliation

					1995
	Movement of cash	Acquisitions less divestments	Non-cash movements	Exchange movements	Balance sheet movement
Inventories	**134**	**33**		**(5)**	**162**
Debtors	**91**	**62**	**32**	**(11)**	**174**
Creditors	**(25)**	**(81)**	**42**	**10**	**(54)**
Provisions for liabilities and charges	**126**	**(20)**	**(143)**	**(18)**	**(55)**
Working capital and provisions movement	**326**	**(6)**	**(69)**	**(24)**	**227**
Cash	**342**	**32**		**28**	**402**
Bank overdrafts	**(1,173)**	**(25)**		**(17)**	**(1,215)**
Finance leases and bills of exchange	**19**	**(3)**		**(3)**	**13**
Loans	**(484)**	**(259)**		**(32)**	**(775)**
Assets held under contract for sale			**34**		**34**
Movement on net debt	**(1,296)**	**(255)**	**34**	**(24)**	**(1,541)**

Other balance sheet items					
Tangible assets	614	27	(415)	21	247
Investments	(29)		(48)	(3)	(80)
Interest	(4)				(4)
Dividends	542		(608)		(66)
Taxation	474	5	(417)	4	66
Minority interests	261	485	(54)	46	738
Total movements	888	256	(1,577)	20	(413)

Returns on investments and servicing of finance

6.10 'Returns on investments and servicing of finance' are receipts resulting from the ownership of an investment and payments to providers of finance, non-equity shareholders and minority interests, excluding those items that are specifically required by the standard to be classified under another heading. [FRS 1 para 13].

6.11 This heading was introduced by the original FRS 1 following the controversy that surrounded the classification of interest and dividends paid in the cash flow statement proposed by ED 54. ED 54 proposed that dividends paid by an enterprise should be classified under financing activities whereas interest received and paid and dividends received should be shown under operating activities. However, many commentators on the exposure draft felt that a reasonable case could be made for an alternative classification as both were payments to providers of capital. As there was no consensus on the preferred treatment both in the UK and internationally, the ASB dealt with the controversy by simply requiring all interest and dividends paid and received to be shown under a separate heading in the cash flow statement. The controversy appears to have resurfaced, although not in the same context as before. The ASB's consultation revealed that there was general support for at least equity dividends paid to be taken out of 'returns on investments and servicing of finance' and located further down the statement after 'acquisition and disposals' on the grounds that such payments are more discretionary than, say, dividends on non-equity shares and interests payments on debt, which have to be made. As a result, equity dividends paid are no longer included under this heading.

6.12 Cash inflows in respect of returns on investments include the following items that should be separately disclosed:

■   Interest received, including any related tax recovered.

■ Dividends received net of any tax credits (except dividends from equity accounted entities whose results are included as part of operating profit).

[FRS 1 para 14].

6.13 Similarly, cash outflows from servicing of finance include:

■ Interest paid (even if capitalised), including any tax deducted and paid to the relevant tax authority.

■ Cash flows that are treated as finance costs under FRS 4 (this will include issue costs on debt and non-equity share capital).

■ The interest element of finance lease rental payments.

■ Dividends paid on non-equity shares of the entity

■ Dividends paid by subsidiaries to equity and non-equity minority interests.

[FRS 1 para 15].

Table 4 below provides a good illustration of the type of items that should be included under returns on investments and servicing of finance.

Table 4 – HSBC Holdings plc – Annual report and accounts – 31 December 1994

**Consolidated Cash Flow Statement
for the Year Ended 31 December 1994 (extract)**

	Note	1994 £m	1993 £m
Net cash (outflow)/inflow from operating activities	35	(1,249)	11,010
Returns on investments and servicing of finance:			
Income received on investment securities		706	630
Dividends received from associated undertakings		43	12
Interest paid on finance leases and similar hire purchase contracts		(11)	(9)
Interest paid on loan capital		(288)	(231)
Dividend paid to minority interests			
- equity		(115)	(109)
- non-equity		(17)	(7)
Ordinary dividends paid*		(254)	(417)
Net cash inflow/(outflow) from returns on investments and servicing of finance		64	(131)

* Under the revised standard ordinary dividends paid would not be shown under this heading.

6.14 Investment income included under this heading will include income from current asset investments, irrespective of whether they are regarded as liquid resources, and on fixed asset investments other than equity accounted entities whose results are included as part of operating profit.

6.15 The standard requires that the cash flow effect of any tax relating to interest should be shown as part of the interest. This applies to tax deducted at source on interest received as well as to tax withheld on interest paid. This means that the actual cash received (or paid) in respect of interest must be shown, but where tax has been deducted at source (or withheld) and is subsequently recovered (or paid), it should also be included under this heading as part of interest received (or paid) at the time of receipt (payment). For example, where there is a timing difference between the actual interest received (or paid) and the settlement of the tax, the net interest received (or paid) would fall to be shown in the period in which the cash is received (or paid), whereas the cash flow effect of any tax deducted at source (or withheld) would fall to be shown in the period in which the tax is recovered (or paid).

6.16   Interest paid should be the actual amount of interest paid during the period, irrespective of whether it is charged to the profit and loss account or capitalised in the balance sheet. Similarly, the interest paid on finance lease obligations should be reported under this heading.

6.17   Unlike the treatment of tax on interest in the cash flow statement, the tax credits on dividends received or the ACT on dividends paid is not reported as part of dividends received or paid. Rather, the net amount of any ACT paid during the period is reported under taxation (see para 6.20 below). This is because under the imputation system of company taxation no withholding tax is actually deducted on dividends paid or tax actually paid on dividends received by a UK company, ACT generally represents an advance payment of tax

6.18   The cash flows relating to finance costs for non-equity shares and debt should be reported under this heading. Therefore, in addition to reporting finance costs such as dividends paid on non-equity shares and interest paid on debt instruments, this heading would also include any payments made for the issue of non-equity shares and debt instruments. Furthermore, the cash flow effects of items such as discounts and premiums on debt instruments and non-equity shares, which are treated as finance costs under FRS 4, would also fall to be included under this heading (see para 11.3).

6.19   The segregation of interest and dividends received and interest paid under the heading 'returns on investments and servicing of finance' is relevant particularly to non-financial companies, as these items are normally shown after operating profit. However, many investment companies and financial institutions show interest received and dividends received in their profit and loss account prior to arriving at their operating profit. Banks and insurance companies also include interest paid in operating profit. Where the special nature of the business requires the inclusion of items relating to interest and dividend in operating profit, the cash flows relating to these items should remain as part of the operating cash flows. If any interest paid clearly relates to financing, then it should be included under 'returns on investments and servicing of finance'. [FRS 1 para 60].

Taxation

6.20 The treatment of taxation cash flows arising from revenue and capital profits proposed in ED 54 was another area that generated a significant amount of controversy. ED 54 proposed that such taxation cash flows should be shown as operating activities unless material elements of cash flows related to investing and financing activities, in which case they should be reported under the relevant headings. Many commentators on the exposure draft felt that, in practice, it may be inappropriate and rather misleading to require allocation between the three economic activities. As payment of corporation tax involves only one cash flow based on taxable income arising from all sources, including chargeable capital gains, and not a collection of individual taxation cash inflows and outflows, any apportionment based on the activities that gave rise to them could in some cases only be done on an arbitrary basis. Consequently, any allocation that attempted to segregate the taxation cash flows in this manner may result in the reporting of hypothetical figures in the cash flow statement. This argument was felt to be sufficiently strong and convincing for the ASB to require all taxation cash flows arising from revenue and capital profits to be disclosed in a separate section within the cash flow statement entitled 'taxation'.

6.21 Reporting entities need to include under this heading the following items in respect of taxation relating to revenue and capital profits:

■　　Cash receipts from the relevant tax authority of tax rebates, claims or returns of overpayments.

■　　Cash payments for corporation tax, including payments of ACT.

For a subsidiary undertaking, payments received from or made to other members of the group for group relief should be included under this heading. [FRS 1 paras 17, 18].

6.22 It should be noted that cash flows relating to VAT or other sales taxes, employees income taxes, property taxes and any other taxes not assessed on revenue and capital profits should not be shown under the heading of 'taxation'. [FRS 1 para 16].

6.23 Generally, payments or receipts of VAT or other sales taxes should be netted against the cash flows that gave rise to them. For example, payments for fixed assets should be shown net of VAT under capital expenditure. However, where the VAT falls to be irrecoverable, because the entity carries on an exempt or partially exempt business, or incurs VAT on items that are disallowed (for example, VAT on purchase of motor vehicles), the cash flows should be shown gross of the irrecoverable tax. If this is not practicable for any reason, the irrecoverable tax should be included under the most appropriate standard heading. [FRS 1 para 39].

6.24 The net movement on the VAT payable to, or receivable from, Customs & Excise should be allocated to cash flows from operating activities unless it is more appropriate to allocate it to another heading. [FRS 1 para 39]. Generally, the majority of the VAT transactions would be relevant to operating activities, but where a significant proportion of the VAT payments (or receipts) relate to other cash flow headings, such as 'capital expenditure and financial investments' or 'acquisitions and disposals', it may be appropriate to include the net payment (or receipt) under that heading. The effect of including the net movement on the VAT account in operating cash flows means that there will be no need to eliminate the amount of VAT included in opening and closing debtors or creditors when carrying out the reconciliation between operating profit and net cash flow from operating activities.

6.25 Taxation cash flows excluding those in respect of tax on revenue and capital profits, VAT or other sales taxes should be included in the cash flow statement under the same standard headings as the cash flow that gave rise to the taxation cash flows. [FRS 1 para 40]. For example, employers' national insurance contributions and amounts paid in respect of PAYE to the tax authorities should be included in operating activities. Where the direct method is followed, they will be included in the amounts shown as paid to or on behalf of employees.

Capital expenditure and financial investment

6.26 'Capital expenditure and financial investment' is a new heading that resulted from the need to split the former 'investing activities' into two new headings, the other being 'acquisitions and disposals' which is considered from paragraph 6.32 below. The cash flows included in 'capital expenditure and financial investment' include the cash effects of transactions relating to the acquisition and disposal of any fixed asset (including investments) and current asset investments not regarded by the enterprise as liquid resources. For this purpose, fixed asset investments exclude a trade or business, or investment in an entity that is an associate, joint venture or a subsidiary undertaking. The cash flows relating to the acquisitions and disposals of these fixed asset investments are reported under 'acquisitions and disposals'. Therefore, cash flows relating to acquisitions and disposals of certain financial investments, for example long-term investments in gilts or other financial investments that are held purely for investment purposes and not for the management of liquid resources, would be reported under this heading, but returns on them would be reported under 'returns on investments and servicing of finance'. If no cash flows relating to financial investments fall to be included under this heading, the caption may be reduced to 'capital expenditure'. [FRS 1 para 19].

6.27 Cash inflows in respect of 'capital expenditure and financial investments' include the following items that should be separately disclosed:'

■   Receipts from sales or disposals of property, plant or equipment.

■   Receipts from the repayment of the reporting entity's loans made to other entities or sale of other entities' debt instruments other than receipts forming part of an acquisition or disposal or a movement in liquid resources.
[FRS 1 para 20].

6.28 Cash outflows in respect of 'capital expenditure and financial investments' include the following items that should be separately disclosed:

■   Payments to acquire property, plant or equipment.

■   Loans made by the reporting entity and payments to acquire debt instruments of other entities other than payments forming part of an acquisition or disposal or a movement in liquid resources.
[FRS 1 para 21].

6.29 The amount paid in respect of tangible fixed assets during the year may not be the same as the amount of additions shown in the tangible fixed asset note. The difference may be due to a number of reasons. For example, tangible fixed assets may be purchased on credit, in which case the amounts for additions shown in the fixed asset note would need to be adjusted for the outstanding credit to arrive at the cash paid. Furthermore, the change in fixed asset creditors should be eliminated from the total change in creditors, to arrive at the movement in operating creditors, a figure needed for the reconciliation of operating profit to net cash flow from operating activities.

Another example is where fixed assets have been acquired in foreign currencies. In this situation, the sterling equivalent of the foreign currency amount paid that is reported in the cash flow statement is not necessarily the same as the sterling equivalent of the cost recorded at the date of the transaction and included in the balance sheet, because of changes in exchange rates. In addition, where interest has been capitalised during the period, the figure for interest would need to be deducted to arrive at the correct amount of cash paid for the acquisition or construction of a fixed asset. The amount of interest capitalised and paid during the period would be shown under 'returns on investments and servicing of finance'.

6.30   A further example arises where assets have been acquired during the year under finance leases. Most companies do not show assets acquired under finance leases separately, but include them in the total additions figure for the year in their fixed assets movements note. Since assets acquired under finance leases do not involve any cash outlay at the inception of the lease, it will be necessary to eliminate the fair value of the leased assets that is included in the figure for fixed assets additions so that the true cash outflow for fixed assets actually purchased can be reflected in the cash flow statements (see worked example, para 12.1). The finance lease rental payments should be analysed between interest and capital, with the interest element shown under 'returns on investments and servicing of finance' and the capital element shown under 'financing'.

6.31   Companies may invest to maintain their existing level of operations (for example, routine replacement of plant and machinery for normal wear and tear) or to expand that level of operations (for example by investing in new products, services or businesses). The original FRS 1 recognised that it may be difficult to distinguish clearly between these two types of capital expenditure in the light of constantly changing technologies, markets and processes, but nevertheless encouraged disclosure where such a distinction could be made. In practice, such disclosures were rarely, if ever, made. So the revised standard neither requires nor encourages their disclosure. However, it does require cash flows to be analysed between capital expenditure and acquisitions and disposals. This is a useful split, but should not be interpreted as reflecting replacement expenditure on the one hand and expenditure for expansion on the other because, depending on circumstances, expansion may be included under either heading.

Acquisitions and disposals

6.32   As already discussed in paragraph 6.31 above, 'acquisitions and disposals' is a new heading that is a subset of the former 'investing activities'. The cash flows under this heading are those related to the acquisition or disposal of any trade, business or an entity that is an associate, joint venture or a subsidiary undertaking. [FRS 1 para 22].

6.33   Cash inflows from 'acquisitions and disposals' include:

■   Receipts from sales of investments in subsidiary undertakings, showing separately any balances of cash and overdrafts transferred as part of the sale (see further para 8.9).

■   Receipts from sales of investments in associates or joint ventures.

■   Receipts from sales of trades or businesses.
[FRS 1 para 23].

6.34   Similarly, cash outflows from 'acquisitions and disposals' include:

■   Payments to acquire investments in subsidiary undertakings, showing separately any balances of cash and overdrafts acquired (see further para 8.9).

■   Payments to acquire investments in associates and joint ventures.

■   Payments to acquire trades or businesses.
[FRS 1 para 24].

Cash flows arising under this standard heading are discussed from paragraph 8.1 dealing with consolidated cash flow statements.

Equity dividends paid

6.35   As explained in paragraph 6.11, equity dividends paid by the reporting entity should be disclosed separately. These are dividends paid on the reporting entity's, or, in a group, the parent's equity shares. For this purpose, equity shares are those that fall to be treated as equity under FRS 4. The dividends paid should be the cash dividend paid and excludes any advance corporation tax. [FRS 1 para 25]. Dividends paid by subsidiaries to shareholders outside the group, both in respect of equity and non-equity interests must be reported under 'returns on investments and servicing of finance'. Therefore, equity dividends paid to minority interests should not be shown under this heading.

Management of liquid resources

6.36 The 'management of liquid resources' is a new heading that arises as a result of the abolition of former 'cash equivalents', which, as already explained in paragraph 2.10, was considered to be the main defect in the original standard. The revision, which drops cash equivalents and changes the focus of the cash flow statement to report only movements in cash, effectively deals with the concerns of company treasurers and others by requiring treasury activities to be reported under this new heading. This heading, therefore, includes cash flows relating to items that were formerly classified as cash equivalents and most liquid items that fell outside cash equivalents and which, by default, were reported as investing cash flows. The type of liquid resources that should be reported under this heading are considered from paragraph 4.5.

6.37 Cash inflows in management of liquid resources include:

■ Withdrawals from short-term deposits not qualifying as cash – to the extent that they do not relate to deposits that qualify for net reporting under a rollover or reissue transaction as explained in paragraph 5.9.

■ Inflows from disposal or redemption of any other investments held as liquid resources.
[FRS 1 para 27].

6.38 Cash outflows in management of liquid resources include:

■ Payments into short-term deposits not qualifying as cash to the extent that they do not relate to deposits that qualify for net reporting under a rollover or reissue transaction as explained in paragraph 5.9.

■ Outflows to acquire any other investments held as liquid resources.
[FRS 1 para 28].

6.39 Only cash flows relating to short-term deposits that are not repayable on demand and, therefore, do not meet the definition of cash would fall to be included under this heading. Generally, the gross cash inflows and outflows should be reported, unless the deposit is one that is continuously rolled over, in which case the net cash flows may be shown as explained further in paragraph 5.9.

6.40   Cash outflows and inflows relating to a wide range of other non-cash current investments would also fall to be reported under this heading provided they are easily and promptly convertible into cash through an active market without curtailing or disrupting the entities business as explained in paragraph 4.9. Although many such current asset investments may qualify as liquid resources, not all of them may be used in the entity's treasury activities. Some current asset investments may be held purely for investment purposes. Others may be held for trading purposes, although this would generally apply to banks and investment companies. Given that there is a choice as to which current asset investment can be used for managing the net funds or net debt position, the standard requires entities to explain what it includes as liquid resources and any changes in its policy. [FRS 1 para 26]. This is a sensible requirement as an investment initially acquired for investment purposes in one year could be designated as a liquid resource in the following year depending on the company's circumstances. A change in policy regarding the use of a particular investment would not give rise to any cash flows in the year of change, but would need to be reported as a non-cash movement in the reconciliation and analysis of net debt (see para 7.1).

6.41   The reporting of cash flows relating to the management of liquid resources is a significant improvement over the original standard as cash flows relating to treasury activities can now be viewed as a whole and kept separate from other investing decisions. The previous practice of reporting large volatile cash flows from short-term investing activities with the normal flows from long-term investing activities relating to the acquisitions and disposals of fixed assets and businesses merely served to distort the investing section of the cash flow statement and was not particularly useful.

Financing

6.42   Financing cash flows comprise receipts from or repayments to external providers of finance. [FRS 1 para 29]. They will generally include the cash effects of transactions relating to the manner in which the operating and investing activities of the enterprise have been financed. However, only cash flows that relate to the principal amounts of finance are dealt with under this heading, since the cash flows relating to the servicing of finance (that is, dividends and interest) are dealt with under returns on investments and servicing of finance heading and equity dividends paid.

6.43   Cash inflows in respect of financing include the following items:

■   Receipts from issuing shares or other equity instruments.

■   Receipts from issuing debentures, loans, notes and bonds, and from other long and short-term borrowings (other than bank overdrafts). [FRS 1 para 30].

6.44   Cash outflows in respect of financing include the following items:

■   Repayments of amounts borrowed (other than overdrafts). The treatment of discounts and premiums on debt instruments is considered in paragraph 11.3 below.

■   The capital element of finance lease rental payments.

■   Payments to re-acquire or redeem the entity's shares.

■   Payments of expenses or commissions on any issue of equity shares. [FRS 1 para 31].

Table 5 shown below provides an illustration of the items that are normally included under this heading.

**Table 5 – Coats Viyella Plc – Report and Accounts –
31 December 1995**

Cash flow statement (extract)

For the year ended 31 December 1995	Notes	1995 £m	1994 £m
Financing			
Issue of ordinary share capital		**(2.6)**	(2.7)
Expenses of enhanced share dividend issues		**-**	0.5
Issues of shares to minorities(see note 26)		**(0.5)**	(3.2)
New long-term loans		**(69.2)**	(0.5)
New short-term loans		**(153.3)**	(77.4)
Repayment of amounts borrowed		**127.2**	113.7
Redemption of convertible debt		**6.7**	-
Capital element of finance lease rental payments		**6.4**	8.3
Net cash (inflow)/outflow from financing		**(85.3)**	38.7

6.45 The cash flows under financing can be shown in a single section with those under 'management of liquid resources', provided that separate subtotals for each are given. [FRS 1 para 29]. The flexibility to report cash flows relating to liquid resources and financing under a combined heading may appeal to a number of companies that manage their borrowings and liquid investments as an integrated treasury operation.

Exceptional and extraordinary cash flows

6.46 Where cash flows relate to items that are classed as exceptional, these exceptional cash flows should be shown under the appropriate standard heading, according to the nature of each item. The exceptional cash flows should be separately identified in the cash flow statement or a note to it and the relationship between the cash flows and the exceptional item should be explained. [FRS 1 para 37].

6.47 FRS 3 requires three exceptional items to be reported after operating profit:

- Profits or losses on the sale or termination of an operation.
- Profits or losses on sale of fixed assets.
- Costs of a fundamental reorganisation or restructuring.

The first two items are not themselves cash flows, but the net cash proceeds from the sale of operations will fall to be included under 'acquisitions and disposals', and those arising from the sale of fixed assets under 'capital expenditure and financial investment', irrespective of where the gain or loss is charged in the profit and loss account (see further paras 11.5 to 11.8).

6.48   The disclosure of cash flows relating to costs of a fundamental reorganisation or restructuring that is reported outside operating profit is not so clear. In general, the cash outflows are likely to include an amalgam of items, such as:

- Redundancy costs.
- Costs associated with the elimination and reduction of product lines.
- Costs to consolidate or relocate plant facilities.
- Costs for new systems developments or acquisition.
- Costs to retrain employees to use newly deployed systems.
- Losses on asset impairments and disposal of assets.

However, as stated in paragraph 6.1 above, the standard makes it clear that the cash flows relating to any operating items should be reported in operating cash flow, whether or not the costs are included in operating profit. This means that the nature of each item included within the total reorganisation costs needs to be analysed, with the result that some cash flows fall to be reported under operating activities, some under capital expenditure and some under acquisitions and disposals.

6.49   The original standard had no clear rules and so in the past the analysis mentioned above was rarely done. Companies tended to include the total cash flow effect of a fundamental reorganisation or restructuring within operating cash flows by disclosing it either separately on the face of the cash flow statement (see Table 6), or showing the amounts expended as a separate line item in the note of the reconciliation of operating profit to net operating cash flows (see Table 7). Given the new requirement that cash flows relating to operating items should be included in operating cash flows, irrespective of where the costs are reported in the profit and loss account, it is doubtful whether companies will be able to use the presentation given in Table 6 and Table 7 without carrying out a proper analysis. The cash flow effect of reorganisation provisions arising on an acquisition of a subsidiary is considered in paragraph 11.9 below.

Table 6 – Imperial Chemical Industries PLC – Annual report and accounts – 31 December 1995

statement of group cash flow (extract)
for the year ended 31 December 1995

	Notes	1995 £m	1994 £m
Cash inflow from operating activities			
Net cash inflow before exceptional items	26	1,277	1,032
Outflow related to exceptional items	27	(86)	(144)
Net cash inflow from operating activities		1,191	888

notes relating to the accounts (extract)

27 Outflow related to exceptional items

This includes expenditure charged to exceptional provisions relating to business rationalisation and restructuring and for sale or closure of operations, including severance and other employee costs, plant demolition and site clearance. The major part of the 1995 expenditure related to provisions raised in 1992 and 1994.

Table 7 – Bass PLC – Annual Report – 30 September 1993

GROUP CASH FLOW STATEMENT (extract)

(I) RECONCILIATION OF PROFIT ON ORDINARY ACTIVITIES BEFORE INTEREST TO NET CASH INFLOW FROM OPERATING ACTIVITIES	1993 £m	1992 £m
PROFIT ON ORDINARY ACTIVITIES BEFORE INTEREST	590	519
Depreciation	180	178
Loss on disposal of fixed assets	10	11
Loss/(surplus) on disposal of operations	3	(3)
Decrease/(increase) in stocks	59	(7)
(Increase)/decrease in debtors	(11)	36
Decrease in creditors	(20)	(64)
Amortisation of and provisions against investments	24	20
Cost of fundamental reorganisation provided	-	75
Provisions expended:		
Acquisition	(41)	(50)
Reorganisation	(44)	(80)
NET CASH INFLOW FROM OPERATING ACTIVITIES	750	635

NOTES TO THE FINANCIAL STATEMENTS (extract)

16 PROVISIONS FOR LIABILITIES AND CHARGES (extract)

Reorganisation provisions were created over a number of years in relation to a major programme of fundamental reorganisation which established the present divisional structure and led to rationalisation within the Brewing, Pubs and Leisure divisions designed in part to reduce the operational cost bases and in part to improve efficiency. Acquisition provisions were created in connection with the purchase of the Holiday Inn Business in North America and Granada Leisure to reflect the costs of integrating these businesses into the Group.

6.50   There may be instances where the cash flows are exceptional because of their size or incidence, but are not related to items that are treated as exceptional in the profit and loss account. These exceptional cash flows should also be disclosed and sufficient explanation given to explain their cause and nature. [FRS 1 para 38]. An example cited in the explanatory paragraph of the standard is that of a large prepayment against a pension liability which is not reported as part of an exceptional or extraordinary item in the profit and loss account. [FRS 1 para 63]. Disclosure of exceptional cash flows where there is no corresponding exceptional item in the profit and loss account is likely to arise where the provision to which the cash flows relates was reported as an exceptional item in a previous period.

6.51   It follows from the requirements explained in paragraphs 6.46 and 6.50 that the cash flow statement should disclose separately any cash flows that are exceptional because of their size or incidence, irrespective of whether or not they relate to items that are reported as exceptional in the profit and loss account. Sufficient disclosure of the nature of the exceptional item and the related cash flows should also be given in a note to the cash flow statement so that users may gain an understanding of how these transactions have affected the reporting entity's cash flows.

6.52   Cash flows from extraordinary items would be reported in a similar manner. [FRS 1 paras 37]. In practice, however, such cash flows will rarely arise, if at all, following the virtual abolition of extraordinary items under FRS 3.

Chapter 7

Reconciliation with balance sheet figures

Reconciliation to net debt

7.1   One of the objectives of the cash flow statement is to provide information that is useful in assessing the liquidity, solvency and financial adaptability of an enterprise. Critics of the original standard argued that this objective was not met by a cash flow statement that focused only on the changes in cash and cash equivalents. Indeed, many companies chose to give additional information that highlighted the movement in net funds or net debt, which they regarded as more useful than the movements in cash and cash equivalents in providing a better indication of the liquidity and solvency of their businesses. In its revision of FRS 1, the ASB acknowledged that the movement in net debt, which is a widely used financial indicator, can provide useful information about changes in liquidity on a broader basis than that provided solely by the movement in cash balances.

7.2   The revised standard, therefore, requires a note that reconciles the movement of cash in the period with the movement in *net debt* for the period. The changes in net debt should be analysed from the opening to the closing component amounts as shown in the opening and closing balance sheets. The reconciliation is not part of the cash flow statement and, if adjoining the cash flow statement (for example, presented at the foot of the statement), it should be clearly labelled and kept separate. [FRS 1 para 33]. For this purpose, net debt is defined to include the borrowings of the reporting entity (comprising debt as defined in FRS 4, together with related derivatives and obligations under finance leases), less cash (including overdrafts) and liquid resources. Where cash and liquid resources exceed the borrowings of the entity, reference should be made to 'net funds' rather than to 'net debt'. [FRS 1 para 2].

7.3   The reconciliation should begin with the increase or decrease in cash for the period as shown at the bottom of the cash flow statement. Because this movement in cash includes cash flows relating to management of liquid resources and cash flows relating to borrowings included in financing, these cash flows should be added back to give the total change in net debt resulting from cash flows during the period. These separate components of cash flows should be separately disclosed in the reconciliation where material. There may be other changes in net debt for the period that do not arise from cash flows. Typically these non-cash movements may relate to items such as exchange differences, acquisition of assets under finance leases, loans and finance leases acquired as part of an acquisition and other movements that have an effect on the closing figure for net debt. These non-cash changes in net debt should also be disclosed in the reconciliation, if material. [FRS 1 para 33]. The way in which this reconciliation should be carried out is shown in the worked example on page 104.

7.4 The total change in net debt arising from both cash flows and non cash items should then be reconciled with the opening and closing net debt amounts. In particular, the standard requires the following reconciling items to be disclosed, where material:

■ The cash flows relating to the separate component of net debt as explained above.

■ The acquisition or disposal of subsidiary undertakings. These relate to borrowings acquired or transferred as part of the acquisition or disposal of a subsidiary undertaking because these are not reflected in the financing section of the cash flow statement, but have an effect on the closing amount of net debt.

■ Other non-cash changes – an example being the acquisition of fixed assets under finance leases.

■ The recognition of changes in market value and exchange rate movements. For example, changes in market values relating to current asset investments that are treated as liquid resources do not have any cash flow impact during the period, but may affect the carrying value of those investments at the balance sheet date (for example, if the company has a policy of marking to market such investments). Similarly, exchange rate adjustments arising from the retranslation of opening foreign currency cash and borrowings and those arising from translating the cash flows of subsidiaries at rates other than the year end rate, do not give rise to any cash flows, but form part of the carrying values of cash and borrowings at the period end.

[FRS 1 para 33].

A similar reconciliation to the one required by the standard is given in Table 8 below.

Table 8 – Kingfisher plc – Annual Report and Accounts –
3 February 1996

CONSOLIDATED CASH FLOW STATEMENT (extract)
Kingfisher plc and subsidiary companies for the year ended 3 February 1996

£million	notes	1996 £m	1995 £m
Reconciliation of net borrowings			
At start of year		**(457.7)**	(355.4)
Increase/(decrease) in cash and cash equivalents		**32.5**	(133.4)
Net sale of investments		**10.9**	25.5
Change in market value of investments		**0.8**	(0.1)
Net (draw down)/repayment of loans		**(72.2)**	25.4
Other non-cash and cash equivalent movements		**(10.6)**	(9.4)
Foreign exchange effects		**(15.6)**	(10.3)
At end of year		**(511.9)**	(457.7)

Analysis of changes in net debt

7.5   Where the opening and closing amounts of net debt shown in the above reconciliation are not readily apparent, because they are included under different balance sheet headings, sufficient details should be shown to enable the cash and other components of net debt to be respectively traced back to the amounts shown under the equivalent caption in the balance sheet. [FRS 1 para 33]. For example, bank loans and overdrafts included as a single figure within current liabilities would need to be identified separately because overdrafts, unlike other borrowings, are included within the cash component of net debt. Another example where separate identification may be necessary relates to the situation where some current asset investments are used for managing liquid resources, but others are not. This additional note is also necessary to enable the movements in net debt for the period to be readily understood. For example, the reclassification of an amount of debt from long term to current categories in the balance sheet would not appear in the reconciliation to net debt, because it is a movement within the same component of net debt, but would need to be separately identified in the analysis of the changes in net debt for the closing amount of current and non-current debt to be readily identified with balance sheet figures. A format for the analysis of net debt, which is based on the example given in the Appendix to the standard, is included in the worked example on page 106.

7.6   It should be noted that the reconciliation of the movement in cash to the movement in net debt and the analysis of changes in net debt effectively combines the notes on the analysis of the changes in cash and cash equivalents, and the analysis of changes in financing that were required by the original standard. Moreover, the reconciliation to net debt and the corresponding analysis note is relevant only to non-financial companies. Banks and insurance companies are not required to give a reconciliation of net debt because the concept of net debt is not really applicable to them. Banks should, therefore, continue to give the notes reconciling the movements in cash and changes in financing with the related items in the opening and closing balance sheet. It should be noted that this requirement for banks is not explicitly stated in the standard, but is illustrated in example 3 in Appendix I to FRS 1. Insurance companies, on the other hand, are required to give an equivalent note that analyses the movement in portfolio investments less financing, either adjoining the cash flow statement or in a note. [FRS 1 para 35]. A note linking the movements to the related balance sheet amounts for portfolio investments and financing is also required. [FRS 1 para 36].

Chapter 8

Consolidated cash flow statements

Introduction

8.1   The form and content of cash flow statements discussed above apply equally to any group of enterprises where consolidated financial statements are prepared. Therefore, a parent company of a group that is required to prepare a consolidated balance sheet and a consolidated profit and loss account should also prepare a consolidated cash flow statement reflecting the cash flows of the group. In preparing consolidated cash flow statements, adjustments should be made to eliminate those cash flows that are internal to the group. Only those cash receipts and payments that flow to and from the group as a whole should be included. [FRS 1 para 43]. Many important issues arise in preparing consolidated cash flow statements and these are considered below.

Minority interests

8.2   Where there are minority interests in any subsidiary that is consolidated as part of a group, the treatment of the minority interest in the consolidated cash flow statement should be consistent with the overall approach followed in preparing the group's financial statements. Companies are required by law and FRS 2 to eliminate intra-group balances and intra-group transactions in the consolidated financial statements. Therefore, they should do the same in preparing a consolidated cash flow statement even where minority interests, which may be substantial, are involved. (For example, where a subsidiary is consolidated because the parent has a participating interest of say 40 per cent and exercises a dominant influence, the minority interest could be 60 per cent.) Intra-group transactions should be eliminated because the group, including partly owned subsidiaries, is a single entity for financial reporting purposes. Therefore, in this situation, only cash flows that are external to the group, which includes those with minorities, should be reflected in the cash flow statements. In particular, the standard requires dividends to minorities to be shown under the heading 'returns on investments and servicing of finance', in the same place as non-equity dividends and separately disclosed.

8.3   FRS 4 requires minority interests to be shown as liabilities where the parent or any fellow subsidiary undertaking has guaranteed their dividends or redemption, or undertaken to purchase the minority shares if the subsidiary fails to make the expected payments. If minority interests are classified as liabilities, the dividends paid on those shares should be shown as part of the interest charge in the consolidated profit and loss account. It follows that, in the consolidated cash flow statement, the dividends paid should similarly be shown as interest paid and not as dividends to minorities; but they would still be included under the heading 'returns on investments and servicing of finance'.

Investments accounted on the equity method

8.4   Where a group has investments in associated undertakings or joint ventures that are included in the consolidation under the equity method, the consolidated cash flow statement should include only the cash flows between the group and those entities, but not the cash flows of those entities. [FRS 1 para 44]. This means that only the following cash flows should be included:

- Cash flows from investments in, and dividends from, the associated undertakings or joint ventures.

- Cash flows from sales or purchases between the group and the associated undertakings or joint ventures.

The same treatment will apply to any non-consolidated subsidiaries that are included in the consolidation using the equity method.

8.5   Specifically, the following information should be disclosed separately for equity accounted entities:

- For equity accounted entities whose results are included as part of operating profits, dividends received from these entities should be included as part of operating cash flows. [FRS 1 para 11]. The difference between dividends received and share of results should be disclosed separately in the reconciliation of operating profit to operating cash flow. [FRS 1 para 12]. See also the worked example at the end of the chapter on page 105.

- For equity accounted entities whose results are reported outside operating profits, dividends received from these entities should be shown under returns on investments and servicing of finance. [FRS 1 para 14(b)].

■   Cash flows relating to acquisitions and divestments should be shown under acquisitions and disposals. [FRS 1 paras 23, 24].

■   Financing cash flows received from or paid to equity accounted entities should be shown under financing. [FRS 1 para 32].

Investments accounted on a proportional basis

8.6   The standard does not specifically deal with investments that are included in the consolidated balance sheet on a proportional basis. The proportional basis of consolidation is sometimes used for non-corporate joint ventures. However, where a joint venture is accounted for on the equity accounting basis the rules in paragraphs 8.4 to 8.5 apply.

8.7   Where a non-corporate joint venture is recorded in the consolidated financial statements using proportional consolidation, the group's proportionate share of that joint venture's cash flows should be included in the consolidated cash flow statement on a line-by-line basis. Therefore, the group's proportionate share of the joint venture's cash flows reported under each of the eight standard headings will be included in the consolidated cash flow statement. Adjustments may have to be made to eliminate cash transactions between the venturer and the joint venture. Separate disclosure is required for cash flows relating to acquisitions and divestments of joint ventures, which should be shown under acquisitions and disposals. [FRS 1 paras 23, 24].

Acquisitions and disposals of subsidiaries

8.8   When a parent undertaking acquires or disposes of a subsidiary undertaking during a financial year, the cash flows relating to the consideration should be reported under acquisitions and disposals in the consolidated cash flow statement.

8.9   The standard specifies the treatment of cash and overdrafts acquired or transferred on acquisition, or disposal, of a subsidiary. It requires that the amounts of cash and overdrafts acquired or transferred to be shown separately along with the gross consideration paid or received for the acquisition or disposal. [FRS 1 paras 23(a), 24(a)]. This is a change from the previous treatment under the original standard that required such amounts to be netted off against the gross consideration. It is hard to understand the basis for such a change. Presumably, the rationale for separate presentation is that the cash and overdraft balances acquired with, or disposed of with, the subsidiary undertaking are part of the subsidiary undertaking's working capital and, therefore, different in substance from the gross cash that is expended or generated by the group in the acquisition and disposal of that undertaking.

8.10 Recording the gross consideration separately along with the cash and overdraft balances transferred means that any fixed assets, working capital excluding cash and overdrafts, and borrowings of the subsidiary at the date of acquisition or disposal would need to be eliminated so as to avoid double counting. For example, stock, debtors and creditors acquired or disposed of would need to be eliminated from the total balance sheet changes in stock, debtors and creditors in the reconciliation of operating profit to operating cash flows. Similarly, borrowings including finance lease obligations taken over or transferred would need to reflected in the reconciliation to net debt and the note that analyses the changes in net debt during the period. The worked example at the end of this chapter shows the disclosure and the adjustments that need to be made for an acquisition (see page 107).

8.11 Where the consideration for the acquisition or disposal has been discharged partly in *cash* and partly by the issue of *shares*, the cash flow statement would show only the cash element of the consideration paid or received. This would be shown as a single item (along with any cash and overdrafts of the subsidiary acquired or disposed of) under the heading 'acquisitions and disposals'. The shares that are issued as part of the consideration in exchange for net assets acquired do not give rise to any cash flows and, consequently, they should not be shown in the cash flow statement, but disclosed as a major non-cash transaction in a note to the cash flow statement (see para 10.1 below).

Example

A parent company pays £20,000 in cash and issues £40,000 in shares and £50,000 in loan notes to acquire a subsidiary with cash balances of £30,000, borrowings of £60,000 and other net assets including goodwill of £70,000.

In this situation, the cash flow statement would show a cash outflow of £20,000 and a cash inflow of £30,000 under acquisitions and disposals, despite it being an acquisition. The loan notes of £50,000 issued and the borrowings of £60,000 acquired would be reported in the reconciliation statement that analyses the changes in the balance sheet amounts making up net debt. The shares and loan notes would be disclosed in the note giving details of material non-cash transactions (see para 10.1). A note summarising the effects of the acquisition indicating how much of the consideration comprised cash is also required (see para 8.13).

8.12   Where acquisitions and disposals take place during a financial year the cash flows of the group should include the cash flows of the subsidiary for the same period as the group profit and loss account includes the subsidiary's results. [FRS 1 para 43]. This is rather obvious, but care should be taken to eliminate all cash flows between the group and the subsidiary acquired or disposed of for the period that the subsidiary is included within the consolidated figures.

8.13   The standard also requires significant amounts of other disclosures to be made in respect of the cash flow effects of a subsidiary acquired or disposed of during the financial year. First, a note to the cash flow statement should show a summary of the effects of acquisitions and disposals indicating how much of the consideration comprised cash. [FRS 1 para 45]. In order to show the effects of the acquisition and disposal fully, it is necessary to disclose separately the assets and liabilities of the subsidiary acquired or disposed of. In practice, the summary of the effects of acquisitions and disposals required by the standard can be combined with that required by the Act and FRS 6. An example of the relevant disclosures is given in Table 9 below.

8.14   Secondly, reporting entities are required to disclose, as far as practicable and where material, the extent to which the amounts reported under each of the standard headings have been affected by the cash flows of the subsidiary acquired or disposed of during the year. This information can be given by segregating cash flows between continuing and discontinued operations and acquisitions. [FRS 1 para 45]. Consequently, users of financial statements will be able to ascertain the amount of the contribution to the group's cash flows that has been made by an acquired subsidiary and how much the group's cash flows have been depleted as a result of a disposal. This information need only be given in the financial statements for the period in which the acquisition or disposal occurs. [FRS 1 para 48]. In practice, it may be difficult, if not impossible, to give this information, particularly where the business of the acquired subsidiary has been integrated with the group. Therefore, unless the post-acquisition cash flows of the acquired subsidiary are clearly identified and segregated, it may be difficult to attribute cash flows as being strictly related to the acquisition. An example where a company has been able to disclose the material effects of an acquisition on the amounts reported under each standard heading is shown in Table 10.

Table 9 – Bowater PLC – Annual Report – 31 December 1993

NOTES TO THE CASH FLOW STATEMENT (extract)

	Acquisitions		Disposals	
IV EFFECTS OF ACQUISITION AND	**1993**	1992	**1993**	1992
DISPOSALS OF SUBSIDIARY				
UNDERTAKINGS AND BUSINESSES	**£m**	£m	**£m**	£m
Tangible assets	**162.7**	144.6	**10.9**	11.2
Business for resale	**13.5**		**13.5**	
Associates	**1.3**	1.5	**0.1**	0.1
Associates goodwill eliminated		(0.7)		
Equity holding in associate	**(16.6)**			
Surplus properties	**0.2**			
Working capital	**44.2**	50.3	**(1.5)**	3.9
Current and deferred taxation	**8.5**	10.2		
Provisions	**(49.5)**	(65.2)	**1.1**	1.5
Cash and cash equivalents	**14.5**	(48.6)	**(2.3)**	(0.1)
Loan capital	**(89.6)**	(176.9)	**(3.0)**	
Finance leases	**(0.3)**	(3.6)		(0.8)
Minority interests	**(1.0)**	(0.3)		
Goodwill	**239.8**	326.0	**47.4**	16.9
Surplus/(deficiency) on disposal	___	___	**10.3**	(0.6)
	327.7	237.3	**76.5**	32.1
Consideration: cash	**312.3**	226.0	**76.5**	32.1
deferred	**26.7**	11.3		
Taxation relief	**(11.3)**	___	___	___
	327.7	237.3	**76.5**	32.1

V ANALYSIS OF MOVEMENTS OF CASH
AND CASH EQUIVALENTS IN RESPECT
OF ACQUISITIONS AND DISPOSALS OF
SUBSIDIARY UNDERTAKINGS AND
BUSINESSES

	1993 £m	1992 £m	1993 £m	1992 £m
Cash consideration	312.3	226.0	76.5	32.1
Cash and cash equivalents	(14.5)	48.6	2.3	0.1
	297.8	274.6	78.8	32.2

Table 10 – Bowater PLC – Annual Report – 31 December 1993

NOTES TO THE CASH FLOW STATEMENT (extract)

III CASH FLOW MOVEMENTS ARISING FROM BUSINESSES ACQUIRED AND
DISPOSED DURING THE YEAR

	1993 £m	1992 £m
Acquisitions:		
Net cash inflow from operating activities	56.4	53.7
Returns on investments and servicing of finance	(4.9)	(3.2)
Taxation paid	(1.4)	(2.3)
Investing activities	(20.2)	(39.2)
Net cash inflow before financing	29.9	9.0

Disposals have not had a material impact.

Chapter 9

Foreign currency

Introduction

9.1 A company n.ay engage in foreign currency operations in two main ways:

■ First, it may enter directly into business transactions that are denominated in foreign currencies.

■ Secondly, it may conduct its foreign operations through a subsidiary, associated company or branch whose operations are based in a country other than that of the investing company or whose assets and liabilities are denominated in a currency other than that of the investing company (a 'foreign enterprise').

9.2 The results of foreign currency transactions and the financial statements of the foreign enterprise will need to be translated into the currency in which the company reports. This translation process should produce results that are compatible with the effect of exchange rate changes on a company's cash flows and its equity. The accounting treatment of foreign currency operations in cash flow statements can be complex and, even though the standard has been revised, there is still little guidance on the subject. The guidance that follow deals with the treatment of exchange differences in individual companies first, followed by their treatment in consolidated financial statements.

Individual companies

9.3 Where an individual company has cash receipts or makes cash payments in a foreign currency, it is consistent with the objectives of cash flow statements that those receipts and payments should be translated into the reporting currency at the rate ruling at the date on which the receipt or payment is received or paid.

9.4 Exchange differences may, therefore, arise because of a rate change between the transaction date (the date at which the transaction is recorded) and the settlement date. Exchange differences also arise where a transaction remains unsettled (that is, not realised in cash) at the balance sheet date and is required to be retranslated at that date. Such differences relate to the retranslation of monetary assets and liabilities.

Settled transactions

9.5   Where a transaction is *settled* at an exchange rate which differs from that used when the transaction was initially recorded, the exchange difference will be recognised in the profit and loss account of the period in which the settlement takes place. To the extent that the settled transaction relates to operations, the gain or loss would be included in arriving at operating profit. This exchange gain or loss would also have the effect of increasing or decreasing the reporting currency equivalent of amounts paid or received in cash settlement. Consequently, no adjustment for the exchange gain or loss is necessary in the reconciliation of operating profit to operating cash flow. Consider the following example:

Example

A UK company was set up in January 19X5 and raised £200,000 by issuing shares. It purchased goods for resale from France in February 19X5 for FF992,500 when the exchange rate was £1 = FF7.94. It entered the purchase in its stock records as: FF992,500 @ 7.94 = £125,000. Under the terms of the contract, the company settled the debt in October 19X5 when the exchange rate was £1 = FF8.58. The amount paid in settlement was: FF992,500 @ 8.58 = £115,676. The company would, therefore, record an exchange gain of £125,000 − £115,676 = £9,324 in arriving at its operating profit for the year.

Assuming that there are no other transactions during the year and the stock remained unsold at the balance sheet date at 31 December 19X5, a simplified cash flow statement is given below:

Cash flow statement		
	£	£
Net cash flow from operating activities		(115,676)
Financing		
Issue of shares		200,000
Increase in cash		84,324
Workings		
Proceeds of share issue	200,000	
Less: payment for stocks	(115,676)	
Increase in cash		84,324

Reconciliation of operating profit to net cash flow from operating activities

Net operating profit	9,324
Increase in stocks	(125,000)
Net cash flow from operating activities	(115,676)

It is obvious that the net cash flow from operating activities comprises the payment of £115,676 for the stock. Because the outstanding creditor for £125,000 was settled during the year for £115,676, the exchange gain of £9,324 is already reflected in the payment and, therefore, no adjustment for the exchange gain is necessary in the reconciliation of operating profit to operating cash flow as illustrated above. Therefore, as a general rule, exchange differences on settled transactions relating to operations will not appear as a reconciling item in the reconciliation of operating profit to net cash flow from operating activities.

In the above example, had the settlement rate of £1 = FF 8.58 been the rate under a forward foreign exchange contract taken out to pay for the stock on the due date, the stock could have been recorded at the forward rate. In that situation, no exchange difference would be reported in the profit and loss account and the amount shown for the stock movement in the reconciliation would be at the forward rate, that is, £115,676.

9.6   Where a settled transaction does not relate to operations and the exchange gain or loss is included in the profit and loss account, but not within operating profit, the exchange gain or loss will be included as part of the cash flows arising from the settlement. An example would be income receivable from a foreign investment. In this situation, the sterling equivalent of foreign cash actually received would be shown under 'returns on investments and servicing of finance', and would include any exchange gain or loss that arises at the time of receipt reported in the profit and loss account below operating profit.

Unsettled transactions

9.7   Where the transaction remains *outstanding* at the balance sheet date, an exchange difference arises as a consequence of recording the foreign currency transaction at the rate ruling at the date of the transaction (or when it was translated at a previous balance sheet date) and the subsequent retranslation to the rate ruling at the balance sheet date. This exchange difference will generally be included in the profit and loss account. Normally such exchange differences arise on monetary items (for example, foreign currency loans, debtors and creditors). In the context of an individual company's operations, these exchange gains or losses will ultimately be reflected in cash flows. However, the way in which they affect the cash flow statement will depend upon the nature of the monetary assets or liabilities, that is, whether they are short term or long term.

9.8   Where they relate to short-term monetary items such as debtors and creditors, no adjustment for the exchange difference arising on their retranslation at the balance sheet date is necessary in the reconciliation of operating profit to net cash flow from operating activities, even though they do not involve any cash flows. This is because increases or decreases in the debtor or creditor balances will include exchange differences on their retranslation at the balance sheet date, and the total movement in debtors and creditors would form an adjusting item in the reconciliation of operating profit to operating cash flows. The effect is that the net cash flow from operating activities will not be distorted by such retranslation differences as illustrated in the following example.

Example

The facts are the same as in the previous example except that at the company's year end 31 December 19X5 the account had not been settled. At 31 December 19X5 the exchange rate was £1 = FF8.25 so that the original creditor for £125,000 would be retranslated at FF992,500 @ 8.25 = £120,303. The gain on exchange of £125,000 − £120,303 = £4,697 would be reported as part of operating profit for the year. The cash flow statement would be as follows:

Cash flow statement	£
Net cash flow from operating activities	Nil
Financing	
Issue of shares	200,000
Increase in cash	200,000
*Represented by closing cash balances	200,000
Reconciliation of operating profit to net cash flow from operating activities:	
Net operating profit	4,697
Increase in stocks	(125,000)
Increase in creditors	120,303
Net cash flow from operating activities	Nil

It is clear that the exchange difference included in operating profit and in the year end creditor balance cancels each other with the result that operating cash flows are not affected. Therefore, as a general rule balance sheet movements in foreign currency trade debtors and creditors, except where they relate to foreign subsidiaries (see example below), will include the impact of exchange differences reported in operating profit and no adjustments for such exchange differences are necessary in the reconciliation.

9.9 Exchange differences on long-term monetary items such as long-term loans would normally be reported as part of the profit or loss for the financial year. To the extent that such differences are included in operating profit, they need to be eliminated in arriving at the net cash flows from operating activities. This is because the actual movement on long-term monetary items which includes the relevant exchange difference is not reported in the reconciliation of operating profit to operating cash flow. Whether or not the exchange differences are reported within operating profit, they should, nevertheless, fall to be included in the reconciliation to net debt and the note that analyses the changes in the balance sheet amounts making up net debt. Consider the following example:

Example

The opening balance sheet at 1 October 19X5 of a company consists of cash of £100,000 and share capital of £100,000. The company takes out a long-term loan on 31 March 19X6 of US$270,000 when the rate of exchange is £1 = US$1.8. The proceeds are immediately converted to sterling, that is, £150,000. There are no other transactions during the year. The exchange rate at the balance sheet date 30 September 19X6 is £1 = US$1.5.

The summarised balance sheet at 30 September 19X6	
	£'000
Cash	250
Long-term loan ($270,000 @ 1.5)	(180)
Net assets	70
Share capital	100
P&L account	(30)
	70

The foreign currency loan having been translated at the rate ruling at the date of receipt to £150,000 (US$270,000 @ 1.8), is retranslated at the balance sheet date to £180,000 (US$270,000 @ 1.5). The exchange loss of £30,000 is recognised in operating profit for the year. The cash is made up of £100,000 received from the share issue and £150,000 received on converting the currency loan immediately to sterling.

Simplified cash flow statement

	£'000
Net cash flow from operating activities	-
Financing	
Receipt of foreign currency loan	<u>150</u>
Increase in cash	<u>150</u>

Notes to the cash flow statement

Reconciliation of operating profit to net cash flow from operating activities

Operating loss	(30)
Adjustment for exchange loss	<u>30</u>
Net cash flow from operating profit	<u>-</u>

Reconciliation on net cash flow to movement in net funds

Increase in cash in the period	150
Cash inflow from increase in debt	(150)
Change in net funds resulting from cash flows	-
Net funds at 1 October 19X5	100
Exchange difference on loan	(30)
Net funds at 30 September 19X6	<u>70</u>

Analysis of net funds

	At 1 Oct 19X5	Cash Flows	Exchange movement	At 30 Sept 19X6
	£'000	£'000	£'000	£'000
Cash	100	150	-	250
Loans	<u>-</u>	(150)	(30)	(180)
Total	<u>100</u>	<u>-</u>	(30)	<u>70</u>

It is apparent from the above illustration that the exchange loss of £30,000 does not have any cash flow effect and, therefore, needs to be eliminated from operating profit. A similar adjustment would be necessary if the loan remains outstanding at 30 September 19X7. However, if the exchange loss of £30,000 is included outside operating profit, for example in 'other interest receivable/payable and similar income/expense', the exchange difference would only fall to be reported in the reconciliation and the analysis of net funds during the year.

9.10   Similarly, where exchange differences arise on the retranslation of foreign currency cash balances, they will not appear in the cash flow statement. This is because they are non-cash movements within the cash balances and will not form part of the increase or decrease in cash for the financial year. They do, however, form part of the reconciliation of opening to closing balances and will, therefore, appear in the reconciliation to net debt and the note that analyses the changes in net debt during the year.

Borrowings used for hedging equity investments

9.11   Where a company has used foreign currency borrowings either to finance, or to provide a hedge against, its foreign equity investments, exchange differences on the borrowings may have been taken directly to reserves in accordance with paragraph 51 of SSAP 20. These exchange differences will have no cash flow impact and will not be included in the cash flow statement or in the reconciliation of operating profit to net cash flow from operating activities. They must, however, be included in the reconciliation to changes in net debt and the note that analyses the changes in net debt during the year (as illustrated in the example above). Similarly, the exchange difference on retranslating the hedged equity investment (taken to reserve) has no cash flow effect.

Group companies

9.12   Where a group conducts part of its business through a foreign entity, different considerations arise from those for individual transactions discussed above. This is because the cash flows of the foreign entity are considered as a whole rather than as a series of single transactions. There are two commonly accepted methods of translation, the temporal method and the closing rate/net investment method. The latter method is generally used for translation purposes, unless the foreign entity's operations are regarded as being more dependent on the economic environment of the investing company's currency, when the temporal method is used (see further chapter 29).

Temporal method

9.13   Under the temporal method, all non-monetary items and profit and loss account items of the foreign subsidiary or branch are translated at the rate ruling on the transaction date or at an average rate for a period if this is not materially different. Where the reporting entity uses the temporal method to translate the financial statements of the foreign enterprise, then the only exchange differences that arise will be those relating to monetary items and these will be reported as part of operating profit.

9.14 By using the temporal method, the consolidated financial statements reflect the transactions of the foreign enterprise as if they had been entered into by the reporting entity itself. Accordingly, the treatment of exchange differences in the consolidated cash flow statement will be similar to that explained above for exchange differences arising in individual companies.

Net investment method

9.15 Under the closing rate/net investment method, the profit and loss account of the foreign entity is translated at the closing rate or at an average rate for the period. [SSAP 20 para 54]. FRS 1 requires that the same rate that is used for translating the results of activities in the profit and loss account of the foreign subsidiary should also be used for translating the cash flows of those activities for inclusion in the consolidated cash flow statement. [FRS 1 para 41]. This means that *all* the cash flows of the foreign subsidiary (not just those arising from its operating activities) must be included in the consolidated cash flow statement using the same exchange rates (average or closing) as were used for translating the results of its activities in the consolidated profit and loss account.

9.16 Where the group uses the closing rate method of translating the financial statements of a foreign entity, then all exchange differences relating to the retranslation of the opening net assets of the foreign enterprise to the closing rate will have been taken directly to reserves. As such exchange differences have no actual or prospective cash flow effect, they will not be included in the consolidated cash flow statement. However, where the opening net assets include foreign currency cash, overdrafts and loan balances then, to that extent, the exchange difference arising on their retranslation at the closing rate for the current period will have been reflected in the closing balances. Such translation differences should not be reported in the cash flow statement itself, but should be included in the effect of exchange rate movements shown as part of the reconciliation to net debt. [FRS 1 para 33(d)].

9.17 Where the group translates the foreign entity's profit and loss account at an average rate, a further translation difference between the result as translated at the average rate and the result translated at the closing rate will have been taken to reserves. This difference will include the exchange rate effect of the movement in foreign currency cash and overdrafts from the average rate to the closing rate. Under FRS 1, this exchange difference will be included with the exchange differences arising on the retranslation of the opening foreign currency cash, overdrafts and loan balances (as stated in the preceding paragraph) in the note that provides a reconciliation between the movements of cash to net debt. [FRS 1 para 33(d)].

9.18   In summary, the treatment specified in the standard has the effect of removing all exchange differences from the cash flow statement that do not have any cash flow impact in the reporting period. The treatment of foreign currency exchange differences in the consolidated cash flow statement can be fairly complex and the following example illustrates the application of the principles discussed above.

Example

Company A, a UK company, whose accounting period ended on 30 September 19X5, has a wholly-owned US subsidiary, S Corporation, that was acquired for US$600,000 on 30 September 19X4. The fair value of the net assets at the date of acquisition was US$500,000. The exchange rate at 30 September 19X4 and 19X5 was £1 = US$2.0 and £1 = US$1.5 respectively. The average rate for the year ended 30 September 19X5 was £1 = US$1.65.

The summarised balance sheet at 30 September 19X4 and 19X5 and an analysis of the retained profit for the year ended 30 September 19X5 of S Corporation, extracted from the consolidation returns, in dollars and sterling equivalents, are as follows:

Balance sheets of S Corporation

	19X5 $'000	19X4 $'000	19X5 £'000 P&L closing	19X5 £'000 P&L average	19X4 £'000
Exchange rate £1 =			$1.50	$1.65	$2.00
Fixed assets:					
Cost (19X5 additions: $30)	255	225	170.0	170.0	112.5
Depreciation (19X5 charge: $53)	98	45	65.3	65.3	22.5
Net book value	157	180	104.7	104.7	90.0
Current assets:					
Investments	250	100	166.6	166.6	50.0
Stocks	174	126	116.0	116.0	63.0
Debtors	210	145	140.0	140.0	72.5
Cash at bank	240	210	160.0	160.0	105.0
	874	581	582.6	582.6	290.5
Current liabilities:					
Bank overdraft	150	-	100.0	100.0	-
Trade creditors	125	113	83.3	83.3	56.5
Taxation	30	18	20.0	20.0	9.0
	305	131	203.3	203.3	65.5
Net current assets	569	450	379.3	379.3	225.0
Loan stock	150	130	100.0	100.0	65.0
Net assets	576	500	384.0	384.0	250.0
Share capital	300	300	150.0	150.0	150.0
Reserves:					
Pre acquisition	200	200	100.0	100.0	100.0
Post acquisition	76	-	50.7	46.1	-
Exchange difference					
Net assets ($500/1.5 − $500/2.0)	-	-	83.3	83.3	-
Increase ($76/1.5 − $76/1.65)	-	-	-	4.6	-
	576	500	384.0	384.0	250.0

Analysis of retained profit for year ended 30 September 19X5

		Closing rate	Average rate
	$'000	£'000	£'000
Operating profit	135	90.0	81.8
Interest paid	(15)	(10.0)	(9.0)
Taxation	(30)	(20.0)	(18.2)
Dividends paid in the year	(14)	(9.3)	(8.5)
Retained profit	76	50.7	46.1

It is further assumed that company A does not trade on its own and its only income is dividends received from S Corporation. The summarised balance sheet of company A at 30 September 19X4 and 19X5 is as follows:

Company A – Balance sheets	19X5	19X4
	£'000	£'000
Investments in subsidiary ($600,000 @ 2.0)	300	300
Cash	208	200
Net assets	508	500
Share capital	500	500
P&L account (dividend received: $14,000 @ 1.75*)	8	-
	458	500
* actual rate on date dividend received		

Where company A uses the closing rate/net investment method, it may use either the closing rate or the average rate for translating the results of S Corporation. The summarised consolidated profit and loss account for the year ended 30 September 19X5 drawn up on the two basis and the summarised consolidated balance sheet at that date are as follows:

Consolidated profit and loss account	£'000	£'000
for the year ended 30 September 19X5	Closing rate	Average rate
Operating profit of S corporation	90.0	81.8
Operating profit of Company A	8.0	8.0
	98.0	89.8
Adjustment – inter company dividend	(9.3)	(8.5)
Net operating profit	88.7	81.3
Interest paid	(10.0)	(9.0)
Taxation	(20.0)	(18.2)
Retained profit	58.7	54.1

Consolidated balance sheet as at 30 September 19X5		
Fixed assets	104.7	104.7
Current assets:		
Investments	166.6	166.6
Stocks	116.0	116.0
Debtors	140.0	140.0
Cash (S Corporation: £160; Company A £208)	368.0	368.0
	790.6	790.6
Current liabilities:		
Bank overdraft	100.0	100.0
Trade creditors	83.3	83.3
Taxation	20.0	20.0
	203.3	203.3
Net current assets	587.3	587.3
Loan stocks	100.0	100.0
Net assets	592.0	592.0
Share capital	500.0	500.0
Reserves:		
Retained profit	58.7	54.1
Exchange difference on opening net assets	83.3	83.3
Exchange difference on P&L account	–	4.6
Goodwill written off ($100,000 @ 2.0)	(50.0)	(50.0)
	592.0	592.0

In the above illustration goodwill has been translated at the rate ruling on the date of acquisition on the grounds that it arises only on consolidation and is not part of the net assets of the foreign enterprise. An alternative treatment is to regard the goodwill as a currency asset which is retranslated at the closing rate. In this situation, an exchange difference would arise on the opening net investment including the goodwill.

Given the above information, the consolidated cash flow statement drawn up in accordance with the exchange rate used in the profit and loss account and the related notes to the cash flow statement are as follows:

Consolidated cash flow statement for the year ended 30 September 19X5	£'000 Closing	£'000 Average
Net cash flow from operating activities	56.7	52.2
Returns on investments and servicing of finance		
Interest paid ($15,000 @ 1.5 and 1.65)	(10.0)	(9.1)
Taxation		
Overseas tax paid ($18,000* @ 1.5 and 1.65)	(12.0)	(10.9)
Capital expenditure		
Purchase of fixed assets ($30,000 @ 1.5 and 1.65)	(20.0)	(18.1)
Management of liquid resources		
Purchase of current asset investments ($150,000 @ 1.5 and 1.65)	(100.0)	(90.9)
Financing		
Issue of loan stock ($20,000 @ 1.5 and 1.65)	13.3	12.1
Decrease in cash	(72.0)	(64.7)
* Overseas tax paid relates to settlement of previous year's liability		

Reconciliation of net cash flow to movement in net funds	£'000 Closing	£'000 Average
Decrease in cash for the period	(72.0)	(64.7)
Cash flow from increase in liquid resources	100.0	90.9
Cash flow from increase in debt	(13.3)	(12.1)
Change in net fund resulting from cash flows	14.7	14.1
Translation difference (see note 2)	29.9	30.5
Movement in net funds in the period	44.6	44.6
Net funds at 1 October 19X4	290.0	290.0
Net funds at 30 September 19X5	334.6	334.6

Notes to the cash flow statement

1 Reconciliation of operating profit to net cash inflow from operating activities		
	Closing rate	Average rate
	£'000	£'000
Operating profit	88.7	81.3
Depreciation ($53,000 @ 1.5 and 1.65)	35.3	32.1
Increase in stocks ($48,000 @ 1.5 and 1.65)	(32.0)	(29.1)
Increase in debtors ($65,000 @ 1.5 and 1.65)	(43.3)	(39.4)
Increase in creditors ($12,000 @ 1.5 and 1.65)	8.0	7.3
Net cash flow from operating activities	56.7	52.2

The movement in working capital in note 1 above could also be obtained by taking the difference between the closing and the opening balance sheet figures and adjusting the result to eliminate the non-cash effects of exchange rate adjustments. But this method is rather cumbersome as illustrated below for stocks:

	Closing rate	Average rate
	£'000	£'000
Stocks at 30 September 19X5 ($174 @ 1.5)	116.0	116.0
Stocks at 30 September 19X4 ($126 @ 2.0	63.0	63.0
Increase in stocks ($48)	53.0	53.0
Exchange difference:		
On opening balance ($126 @ 1.5 – $126 @ 2.0)	(21.0)	(21.0)
On movement ($48 @ 1.5 – $48 @ 1.65)	-	(2.9)
Increase in stocks included in reconciliation above	32.0	29.1

2 Analysis of net funds – Closing rate method

	1 Oct 19X4 £'000	Cash flow £'000	Exchange difference £'000	30 Sep 19X5 £'000
Cash				
Cash at bank	305.0	28.0	35.0	368.0
Bank overdraft	-	(100.0)	-	(100.0)
	305.0	(72.0)	35.0	268.0
Liquid resources				
Current asset investments	50.0	100.0	16.6	166.6
Debt				
Loan stock	(65.0)	(13.3)	(21.7)	(100.0)
Net funds	290.0	14.7	29.9	334.6

Analysis of net funds – Average rate method

	1 Oct 19X4 £'000	Cash flow £'000	Exchange difference £'000	30 Sep 19X5 £'000
Cash				
Cash at bank	305.0	26.2	36.8	368.0
Bank overdraft	-	(90.9)	(9.1)	(100.0)
	305.0	(64.7)*	27.7	268.0
Liquid resources				
Current asset investments	50.0	90.9	25.7	166.6
Debt				
Loan stock	(65.0)	(12.1)	(22.9)	(100.0)
Net funds	290.0	14.1	30.5	334.6

* Note:

Movements in cash – (S Corp $30 @ 1.65 = £18.2 + A Ltd £8)	£26.2
Movement in overdraft (S corp $150 @ 1.65)	£90.9

See workings below for calculation of exchange differences

The effect of foreign exchange rate changes on net funds may be reconciled as follows.

	Closing rate £'000	Average rate £'000
Cash at bank		
Opening balance ($210 @ 1.5 – $210 @ 2.0)	35.0	35.0
Increase in the period ($30 @1.5 – $30 @ 1.65)	-	1.8
	35.0	36.8
Bank overdraft		
Opening balance	-	-
Increase in the period ($150 @ 1.5 – $150 @ 1.65)	-	(9.1)
	-	(9.1)
Liquid resources – current asset investment		
Opening balance ($100 @ 1.5 – $100 @ 2.0)	16.6	16.6
Increase in the period ($150 @ 1.5 – $150 @ 1.65)	-	9.1
	16.6	25.7
Debt – loan stock		
Opening balance ($130 @ 1.5 – $130 @ 2.0)	(21.7)	(21.7)
Increase in the period ($20 @ 1.5 – $20 @ 1.65)	-	(1.2)
	21.7	(22.9)

9.19 As can be seen from the above example, in practice, a reporting entity will find it simpler to require each of its foreign subsidiaries to prepare a cash flow statement with supporting notes, in its domestic currency. This cash flow statement can then be translated into sterling either at the average rate or the closing rate, whichever rate is used for translating the profit and loss account of the foreign subsidiary for consolidation purposes. The sterling equivalent of each subsidiary's cash flow statement can then be consolidated with the cash flow statement of the reporting entity after eliminating intra-group items such as dividends and inter-group loans.

Intra-group transactions

9.20 Transactions between members of a group located in different countries may not cancel out on consolidation because of exchange differences. As explained in chapter 29, these exchange differences are usually reported in the consolidated profit and loss account, particularly if they relate to intra-group trading transactions and dividends. Such exchange differences may have an effect on group cash flows. For consolidated cash flow statements, these intra-group cash flows may not cancel out unless the actual rate at the date of transfer is used for translation. In the previous example, the only intra-group transaction that took place between the parent and the subsidiary was in respect of a dividend payment. The consolidated operating profit after cancellation of the inter-company dividend is shown below for the two situations where the subsidiary's profit and loss account has been translated at the closing rate and the average rate.

Consolidated profit and loss account for the year ended 30 September 19X5	£'000 Closing rate	£'000 Average rate
Operating profit of S corporation	90.0	81.8
Operating profit of Company A	8.0	8.0
	98.0	89.8
Adjustment – inter-company dividend	(9.3)	(8.5)
Net operating profit	88.7	81.3

9.21 As can be seen the amount of £9,300 and £8,500 is used to cancel the dividend paid by the subsidiary and not the £8,000 received by the parent. It would, therefore, appear that an exchange difference has been left in operating profit, which would need to be eliminated in the reconciliation of operating profit to operating cash flow. However, this is not the case. Deducting the amount for the dividend paid by the subsidiary in the consolidated profit and loss account at the same amount included in the subsidiary's profit and loss account translated at closing rate or average rate, cancels the dividend paid, and so ensures that the consolidated profit and loss account reflects the dividends received by the parent at the sterling amount received. In the consolidated cash flow statement, the same approach is adopted. In effect, the subsidiary's cash flows are reported at the closing rate or average rate, except that the dividend payment is reversed at that same rate and included at the sterling amount actually received by the parent. As a result, no further adjustment for the exchange difference is necessary in the reconciliation of operating profit to operating cash flow, or in the reconciliation to net debt. Indeed, this is to be expected as the transaction was settled during the year, any exchange difference already being reflected in cash flows. The standard, therefore, permits the use of an actual rate, or an approximation thereto, to translate intra-group cash flows in order to ensure that they cancel out in the preparation of the consolidated cash flow statement. [FRS 1 para 41].

9.22   If, on the other hand, the amount of £8,000 received by the parent had been used to cancel the intra-group dividend, the consolidated operating profit would have increased as shown below.

Consolidated profit and loss account	£'000	£'000
for the year ended 30 September 19X5	Closing rate	Average rate
Operating profit of S corporation	90.0	81.8
Operating profit of Company A	8.0	8.0
	98.0	89.8
Adjustment – inter-company dividend	(8.0)	(8.0)
Net operating profit	90.0	89.8

9.23   Using identical amounts to cancel the intra-group dividend in the consolidated profit and loss account does not mean that the exchange difference has been eliminated in the cash flow statement. The effect of using the actual amount received in the cancellation process means that the profits remitted by the subsidiary are being translated at the closing rate or the average rate. As a result the intra-group dividend paid and received does not cancel out in the consolidated cash flow statement. The difference of £1,300 for the closing rate or £500 for the average rate then needs to be eliminated. The standard states that if the rate used to translate intra-group cash flows is not the actual rate, any exchange rate differences should be included in the effect of the exchange rate movements shown as part of the reconciliation to net debt. [FRS 1 para 41]. It could be argued that it makes more sense to report this exchange rate difference in the reconciliation of operating profit to operating cash flows. This is because the subsidiary's cash has gone down by £9,300 and the holding company's cash has gone up by £8,000, resulting in a real economic loss to the group which normally falls to be recognised in the consolidated profit and loss account. However, the treatment required by the standard ensures that the profit and loss account and the cash flow statement are treated in a consistent way. Because, in the above example, operating profit does not include any exchange difference on the intra-group dividend, it follows that no adjustment for the exchange difference is necessary in the reconciliation of operating profit to operating cash flows. The only other place to report this exchange difference is in the reconciliation to net debt.

Hedging transactions

9.24   Hedging transactions are normally undertaken by entities to protect themselves from financial loss, especially loss that would occur if prices or exchange rates were to vary. For example, an entity may purchase or sell a hedging instrument, such as a futures contract or a forward contract, in order to protect itself from price fluctuations that may arise in connection with the sale or purchase of stocks. The question arises as to how cash flows that result from the purchase or sale of the hedging instrument should be classified in the cash flow statement. Should these be shown under capital expenditure and financial investments or classified in the same category as the cash flows of the items being hedged, for example, under operating activities?

9.25   The standard provides that cash flows that result from transactions undertaken to hedge another transaction should be reported under the same standard heading as the transactions which are the subject of the hedge. [FRS 1 para 42]. This is a sensible treatment because it links the cash flows from hedging instruments that are accounted for as hedges with the cash flows arising from the items being hedged. The treatment required by the standard for hedging transactions applies only to futures contracts, forward contracts, options and swaps that are taken out as hedges of identifiable transactions or events. For example, the reporting entity may purchase a futures contract in order to reduce its exposure to increases in the price of a planned stock purchase and, therefore, any cash flows arising on the futures contract should be reported in operating cash flows. It should be noted that the ASB has decided to take a pragmatic approach on hedging because it is currently working on a project on derivatives which will consider all aspects of hedging.

9.26   The treatment required by the standard for hedged transactions cannot apply to situations where the reporting entity hedges a net investment in a foreign subsidiary with a borrowing that is denominated in the same currency as the net investment being hedged (the hedged situation explained in SSAP 20). Accounting for the borrowing as a hedge is incidental; it cannot change the basic fact that it is still a borrowing. Furthermore, the foreign subsidiary may have contributed to group cash flows reported under each of the standard headings. Since the cash flows from the borrowings cannot be identified with any specific cash flows from that subsidiary, it follows that the cash flows from the borrowing can only be classified in the cash flow statement under financing.

Chapter 10

Notes to the cash flow statements

Specific disclosures

10.1 In addition to the cash flow statement itself, the standard requires a number of explanatory notes to the cash flow statements. The positioning of these notes within the financial statements varies from company to company, but in general they are either presented immediately after the cash flow statement itself or are included in the notes to the financial statements with appropriate cross-references to the cash flow statement. Many of the specific disclosures that are necessary to supplement the information presented in the cash flow statement have already been discussed and illustrated by practical examples, but are restated below for completeness.

- A note showing the reconciliation between operating profit and net cash flow from operating activities should be provided. This reconciliation should disclose all differences between operating cash flows and operating profits (see para 6.6). This reconciliation should be presented either adjoining the cash flow statement or in a note to the statement.

- A reconciliation of the movement in cash to the movement in net debt should be provided showing the changes in net debt during the year and the way in which such changes are related to the opening and closing balance sheet figures. This reconciliation, like the previous one, may be presented either adjoining the cash flow statement or in a note to the statement. Where several balance sheet items or parts thereof have to be combined to permit a reconciliation, sufficient detail should be shown to enable the movements to be understood. This detail should be given in a note to the statement (see para 7.5).

- Where a group acquires or disposes of a subsidiary undertaking, the notes to the cash flow statements should show a summary of the effects of the acquisition or disposal. Disclosure should also be made of the extent to which the amounts reported under each of the standard headings have been affected by the cash flows of the subsidiary acquired or disposed of during the year (see paras 8.13 and 8.14).

■ Major non-cash transactions should also be disclosed. Such transactions do not involve any cash flow, but have the same effect as if several cash transactions were made together. For example, conversion of debt to equity can be viewed as the equivalent of repaying debt in cash and then receiving cash on the issue of new shares. Because there are no actual cash flows, the transaction would not feature in the cash flow statement. But important information would thereby remain undisclosed merely because, in effect, a notional cash outflow has been cancelled by an equal and opposite notional cash inflow. Therefore, in order to report the activities of an enterprise in full, material non-cash transactions should be disclosed in a note to the cash flow statement if disclosure is necessary for an understanding of the underlying transactions.

Supplementary disclosures

10.2   In addition to the specific disclosures identified above, the standard *encourages* reporting entities to provide additional information relevant to their particular circumstances. [FRS 1 para 56]. The additional information that may be presented is considered below.

Reporting of gross operating cash flows

10.3   Entities are allowed to provide information on gross operating cash receipts and gross operating cash payments. [FRS 1 para 7]. Clearly, presentation of such information produces a cash flow statement in its purest form with new information that is not otherwise available from the profit and loss account or the balance sheet. The way in which such information should be presented is illustrated in Table 2 above on page 32.

Cash flows from discontinued operations

10.4   Entities are encouraged to distinguish between net cash flows from continuing operating activities and those arising from discontinued operations. [FRS 1 para 56]. Although not specifically required in the standard section of FRS 1, the analysis is given in example 2 of the illustrative examples included in the FRS. This disclosure is consistent with the separate disclosure in the profit and loss account of the results of continuing activities from those relating to discontinued operations required by FRS 3. Many companies have not given this analysis, but one company that has separately reported the cash flows from discontinued operations is BOC Group plc as shown below in Table 11

Table 11 – The BOC Group plc – Report and Accounts – 30 September 1993

CONSOLIDATED CASH FLOW STATEMENT (extract)
YEARS ENDED 30TH SEPTEMBER

		NOTES	1993 £ million	1992 £ million
OPERATING	Net cash flow from continuing operations		**583.9**	563.6
ACTIVITIES	Net cash flow from discontinued operations		–	13.7
	Net cash inflow from operations	3	**583.9**	577.3

Commentary on cash flows in operating and financial review

10.5   It is acknowledged that the assessment of liquidity, viability and financial adaptability of an enterprise requires more information than just a statement of cash flows. The provision of such additional information is now recommended by the ASB's voluntary statement 'Operating and financial review' (OFR). The OFR provides opportunities for listed companies and other large corporations where there is a public interest in their financial statements to provide a commentary on their cash flows. The OFR recommends discussion in the 'financial review' section of 'funds from operating activities and other sources of cash' and 'current liquidity'. Many companies have taken advantage of this opportunity to provide further information on their cash generating potential and liquidity position that go beyond that required by the standard. An example is given in Table 12 below.

Table 12 – THORN EMI plc – Annual Report – 31 March 1996

Financial review (extract)

Cash flow and borrowings

Borrowings increased from £363.3m at 31 March 1995 to £391.4m at 31 March 1996. The principal factors were the inflow of free cash of £159.8m which more than covered the outflow of £143.4m on dividends. However, this net inflow was more than offset by a foreign exchange translation increase of £44.8m which resulted from our policy of protecting shareholders' funds by hedging foreign currency assets with foreign currency borrowings.

Several movements contributed to the £43.1m reduction in free cash flow compared to 1995. The detail of the free cash inflow of £159.8m is shown in the table below. On the positive side, operating profit was £191.5m higher and fixed asset disposals increased by £42.3m. On the negative side, non-cash movements were lower reflecting the higher level of operating exceptional provisions taken in 1995, and provision utilisation was £23.2m higher due to spend on the withdrawal from UK electrical retailing.

Working capital increased by £131.4m, due largely to significant shipments by EMI Music in late March, settlement of the Dillons trade creditors, and a reduction in creditors as a result of the withdrawal from electrical retailing in the UK. Capital expenditure was £35m higher, mostly in EMI Music as it continued to invest in additional CD capacity and IT systems. Finally, tax payments grew by £45.2m as a consequence of both increased profit and the higher tax rate.

Free cash flow

	1996 £m	1995 £m
Operating profit	**520.0**	328.5
Non-cash movements	**579.7**	616.2
Provisions utilised	**(101.8)**	(78.6)
(Increase) decrease in working capital	**(58.7)**	72.7
Net cash inflow from operating activities	**939.2**	938.8
Capital expenditure	**(687.7)**	(652.2)
Sale of tangible fixed assets	**123.0**	80.7
Interest	**(34.9)**	(36.8)
Taxation	**(175.8)**	(130.6)
Other	**(4.0)**	3.0
Free cash flow	**159.8**	202.9
Free cash flow per share	**37.2p**	47.6p

10.6 In discussing the cash generated from operations and other cash inflows during the period, the OFR encourages companies to disclose and discuss segmental cash flows where they are significantly out of line with segmental profits, because of the impact of capital expenditure. [OFR para 31]. In fact, FRS 1 also encourages enterprises to give a segmental breakdown of their cash flows, but does not specify how this information should be given. [FRS 1 para 8]. Many companies, following SSAP 25, 'Segmental reporting', already give segmental information about their operations in terms of turnover, profits, capital employed, etc. The extension of segmental information to cash flows enables users to understand the relationship between the cash flows of the business as a whole and those of its component parts.

10.7 The type of segmental cash flow information that should be reported is not specifically identified by FRS 1 or the OFR, but ED 54 proposed that, as a minimum, an entity should give an analysis of the most important elements of operating cash flows between the major reportable segments. Clearly, there may be problems of allocation, such as common costs and interest, but they could be allocated between segments in the same way as other segmental information. Guidance on the allocation of common costs and interest is given in SSAP 25.

10.8 Some companies are also disclosing 'cash flow per share' (see Table 12 above where Thorn EMI has disclosed an amount for free cash flow per share). Although ED 54 did not recommend the disclosure of cash flow per share on the grounds that it could be regarded as comparable to earnings per share and could be regarded as a substitute for it, there is, in principle, nothing wrong with disclosing this information. Indeed, there is no such prohibition in FRS 1. Cash flow per share information presented over time would reveal the trend of cash flows and, when compared to earnings per share, would demonstrate the quality of profits earned.

10.9 In discussing current liquidity, the OFR calls for disclosure and comments on the level of borrowings including seasonality, peak borrowing levels and maturity profile of both borrowings and committed borrowing facilities. [OFR para 32]. At present, financial statement disclosure about actual borrowings at the year end is provided by analysing bank and other borrowings by maturity period of up to one year, one to two years, two to five years and beyond five years. However, there is no requirement to disclose the amount of undrawn borrowing facilities (both committed and uncommitted). Disclosure of an entity's borrowing facilities together with its ability to access further resources will, no doubt, go a long way in providing useful information about the entity's viability and financial adaptability. However, the level of disclosure is left entirely to the company for obvious reasons. For example, companies could resist such disclosure on the grounds that it provides too much competitive information. Also the company's main bankers could object because disclosure may provide competitors with valuable information on their lending policies.

10.10 The discussion on borrowings suggested by the OFR should also refer to any restrictions on the ability of the group to transfer funds from one part of the group to another and restrictions and breaches of borrowing covenants. [OFR paras 34, 35]. The disclosure of the amounts of cash that are not freely remittable to the parent company coupled with sufficient information on the restrictions (for example, exchange controls) provides useful information for users of financial statements to make an assessment of the probable future effect of the restriction on the company's cash flows. As discussed in paragraph 10.11, the revised standard has now introduced required disclosures on the treatment of cash that is subject to restriction. Similarly, information on assets and liabilities denominated in foreign currencies, which incidentally is not directly relevant for supplementing information reported in the cash flow statement, may be useful for making assessments of a company's liquidity and financial viability. Information on any restrictive financial covenants on current borrowing agreements and breaches or likely breaches of covenants is equally important in assessing its viability and financial adaptability.

Restrictions on remittability

10.11 Sometimes cash may be held in a separate blocked account or an escrow account to be used only for a specific purpose, or held by subsidiaries operating in countries where exchange control restrictions are in force such that cash is not freely transferable around the group. The standard requires that where restrictions prevent the transfer of cash from one part of the business or group to another, a note to the cash flow statement should disclose the amount and explain the nature of the restriction. [FRS 1 para 47]. This is consistent with that recommended by the OFR as discussed in paragraph 10.10 above. However, disclosure is required only in circumstances where the restriction is imposed by external factors outside the company's control. Restrictions arising from a specific purpose designated by the reporting entity need not be disclosed. A typical example of disclosure is where a foreign subsidiary is prevented from remitting funds to its overseas parent, because of local exchange control regulations. [FRS 1 para 68]. Other examples given in the standard where disclosure may be relevant, depending on the regulatory environment, relate to cash balances in escrow, deposited with a regulator or held within an employee share ownership trust. The treatment of cash subject to restriction is considered from paragraph 11.13.

Comparative figures

10.12   Comparative figures should be given for all items reported in the cash flow statements and in the supplementary notes. Comparative figures are required for the reconciliation of the movement of cash to the movement in net debt, but not for the note that analyses the changes in the balance sheet amounts making up net debt. Nor are comparative figures required for the amounts included under each of the standard headings in respect of the cash flows of subsidiaries acquired or disposed of during the year. [FRS 1 para 48].

10.13   Normally, it is a relatively simple matter to provide comparative figures for all items reported in the cash flow statement itself. However, disclosure of comparative amounts for all items reported in the notes to the cash flow statement may cause some practical difficulties in interpreting this requirement. For example, the illustrative example in the standard provides a detailed breakdown of the assets and liabilities of subsidiaries acquired or disposed of during the year, together with an analysis of the net consideration paid or received in the transfer. Normally, such disclosures are also required by the Act and FRS 6, but only in the year of acquisition or disposal. If the strict wording of the standard is to be followed, then comparative figures would be required. Many companies do not provide such comparative information, although it is arguable that where an acquisition or disposal has taken place both in the current and the preceding year, the analysis of the net consideration should be given for both years in the notes as illustrated in Table 9 above on page 62.

Chapter 11

Practical application of FRS 1

Introduction

11.1   This section attempts to clarify some of the practical problems that may arise in interpreting and applying the revised standard. Although the revision of the standard has eliminated many of the problems encountered previously, nevertheless there are some issues that require consideration. No doubt others will arise in due course when companies have become accustomed to the new standard.

Balance sheet cash versus FRS 1 cash

11.2   The strict definition of cash used for the purposes of cash flow reporting explained in paragraph 4.2 above is unlikely to accord with the interpretation of cash used in the balance sheet classification 'cash at bank and in hand'. Although some companies follow a narrow interpretation of cash by including only cash held in current accounts and short-term deposits repayable on demand (former cash equivalents) under the balance sheet heading, others follow a wider interpretation by including the total amount of money on deposit with a bank or financial institution without regard to whether the deposit was short or long term. If the wider interpretation was followed previously, the movements in cash as reported in the cash flow statement are now unlikely to agree with the movements in cash as disclosed in the balance sheet caption, because of the narrow definition of cash included in the revised standard. The differences are likely to be for those short-term deposits that are regarded as liquid resources and whose movements are reported under 'management of liquid resources' and for other long-term deposits that are not regarded as liquid resources whose movements are reported under 'capital expenditure and financial investment'. It may be that following the revision of FRS 1, some companies may change their balance sheet presentation of cash to accord with the strict definition used in the standard. It may also be that companies generally will use the term 'liquid resources' as a new item within the balance sheet classification of current asset investments.

Discounts and premiums

11.3   Where a deep discounted bond is redeemed or a premium is paid on the redemption of a debt security, the question sometimes arises as to where in the cash flow statement the premium should be reported. An intuitive response may be to include it within financing together with the other principal amount repaid on the instrument. However, under FRS 4 the discount on issue and the redemption premium form part of the finance cost of the instruments, which is reported in the profit and loss account as interest expense over the life of the instruments. The revised standard takes a similar approach. It requires that the cash flow effects of these items should be reported within 'returns on investments and servicing of finance' when the instruments are redeemed in order to provide a link between the profit and loss account and the cash flow statement as illustrated in the following example.

Example

A company issues a ten-year zero coupon bond with a face value of £100,000 at a discount of £61,446. Its issue price is, therefore, £38,554 and the effective yield is 10%. How should the transaction be reflected in the cash flow statement?

At the issue date, the proceeds of £38,554 would be shown as a cash inflow in financing. The discount of £61,446 represents a rolled-up interest charge which would be amortised to the profit and loss account as an interest expense over the life of the bond while the bond remains outstanding. However, there would be no cash flow in these periods, because no cash has been paid.

On maturity, the discount of £61,446, which is part of the finance cost under FRS 4, should be shown under 'returns on investments and servicing of finance' separately classified, if material, as premium paid on redemption of bond in accordance with paragraph 15(a) of the standard. The balance of £38,554 should be shown under financing as repayment of the bond. The result is that a decrease in cash of £100,000 would be reported at the end of the cash flow statement. It should be noted that although the discount has been accrued over the years when the bond was in issue, the repayment of the discount on redemption means that the accrual should be adjusted as a non-cash change in the reconciliation to net debt as shown below:

Reconciliation to net debt	£'000
Decrease in cash in the period	(100,000)
Cash flow from decrease in debt financing	38,554
Change in net debt from cash flows	(61,446)
Other non cash changes – reversal of accrual for discount	61,446
Movement in net debt for the period	-

Opening net funds (say cash of £150,000 less bond of £100,000)	<u>50,000</u>
Closing net funds (cash of £50,000)	<u>50,000</u>

It is clear from the above example that accruals for finance costs would need to be reported as other non-cash changes in the reconciliation to net debt. This adjustment should be made both in the year(s) in which the accrual arises (as an increase in net debt) and in the year in which it reverses, otherwise the movement in net debt for the period cannot be reconciled with the opening and closing component of net debt.

A similar treatment would apply to the investor. The investor should record the payment for the bond of £38,554 as part of cash outflow in financial investment. On maturity, the receipt of £100,000 should be split and shown as to £38,554 under financial investment and £61,446 under 'returns on investments and servicing of finance'.

11.4   Where debt instruments are redeemed at a premium, it will also be necessary to separate the principal and the interest element of the amounts paid on redemption. For example, where supplemental interest is paid on convertible bonds that are redeemed rather than converted, the whole amount of the supplemental interest accrued over the life of the bond and paid at redemption should be reported under 'returns on investments and servicing of finance'. Similar arguments would apply to non-equity shares that are redeemed at a premium.

Gains and losses

11.5   It is consistent with the objective of cash flow reporting that gains and losses that do not give rise to any cash flows should be excluded from the cash flow statement. Gains and losses are reported in the profit and loss account or in the statement of total recognised gains and losses of the reporting entity. To the extent that these are included in arriving at operating profit, they should be adjusted (gains should be deducted and losses added) in the reconciliation to arrive at the net cash flow from operating activities. For example, a gain on the sale of plant and machinery that has been included in operating profit (as a depreciation adjustment) should be excluded from cash flow from operating activities. The gain is not a cash flow as such, but forms part of the proceeds from the sale that are disclosed under capital expenditure in the cash flow statement.

11.6   A similar treatment would apply to gains and losses on investments. However, where investments are used for trading activities (typically by a bank or a financial institution), any gain or loss arising on their disposal during the year would be included in operating profit. In this situation, operating profit need only be adjusted for the movement in investments and not for the gain or loss arising (which is realised) to arrive at the net cash flow from operating activities.

11.7   Gains and losses on current asset investments that are regarded as liquid resources, would need to be eliminated from operating profit, if the gain or loss is also reported as part of operating profit, to give the correct cash flow from operating activities. Irrespective of whether or not the gain or loss is reported within operating profit, the gain or loss would need to be reported as a non-cash item in the reconciliation to net debt.

11.8   In relation to debt securities, a further question arises as to whether a gain or loss that arises on the early settlement of a debt security issued by a reporting entity should be reported as part of the finance cost under 'returns on investments and servicing of finance' or as part of the capital repayment under 'financing'. Consider the following example.

Example

The facts are the same as in the previous example except that the company has decided to redeem the bond early at the beginning of year 4 for £55,000.

The carrying value of the bond in the balance sheet at the end of year 3 is calculated as follows:

	£'000	£'000
Proceeds at beginning of year 1		38,554
Interest accrued in year 1 – 10% on £38,554	3,854	
Interest accrued in year 2 – 10% on £42,408	4,241	
Interest accrued in year 3 – 10% on £46,649	4,665	12,760
Carrying value (capital value of bond £100,000 less unamortised discount of £61,446 – £12,760 = £48,686)		51,314
Loss on redemption:		
Redemption payment		55,000
Less carrying value		51,314
		3,686

The loss should be allocated to interest paid, giving £16,446 (£12,760 + £3,686) to be reported under returns on investments and servicing of finance and £38,554 to be reported as capital repayment under financing. This treatment is appropriate because the total cash cost of the finance is reflected in the cash flow statement. Under FRS 4, the difference between the net proceeds of an instrument (in this example, £38,554) and the total amount of the payments made (£55,000) is finance cost (£16,446). As explained before, FRS 1 also requires the cash flow effect to be treated in a similar way. The alternative of reporting the loss incurred as part of the capital repayment, giving £42,240 (£38,554 + £3,686) to be reported under financing and £12,760 to be reported as interest paid under returns on investments and servicing of finance, is not considered acceptable.

Reorganisation costs following an acquisition

11.9   Where a company undertakes to reorganise the business of a recently acquired subsidiary, it may incur costs that are provided for in periods prior to the actual disbursement of cash. The question arises as to whether the subsequent cash outflow in respect of the amount provided should be disclosed as part of operating activities or 'acquisitions and disposals'.

11.10   Prior to the issue of FRS 7, 'Fair values in acquisition accounting', in September 1994, such costs were often provided for as part of the fair value exercise on acquisition, but FRS 7 now requires them to be reported in the post acquisition profit and loss account of the acquiring group. The cash outflows should, therefore, be reported under operating activities if such costs are also reported in the post acquisition profit and loss account in arriving at operating profit. Where the costs are reported as a non-operating exceptional item in accordance with FRS 3 and FRS 6, 'Acquisition and mergers', (that is, if the reorganisation is fundamental to the enlarged group), the exceptional cash flows would also fall to be reported separately under operating activities as discussed in paragraph 6.49 above.

Refinancing of borrowings

11.11   Companies may renegotiate their existing borrowings on terms that are different from those that were in place prior to the renegotiation. For example, as part of the renegotiation, a significant part of the company's current overdraft balance may be converted into a long-term loan. The question arises as to how such a reclassification should be dealt with in the cash flow statement.

11.12   The answer depends on whether the renegotiation gives rise to any cash flows. If the renegotiation is undertaken with the same bankers, it is likely that no cash flows are involved. In that situation, the proper treatment would be to reclassify the relevant portion of the overdraft balance from cash to financing in the notes that analyse the changes in net debt during the year. On the other hand, if the refinancing is carried out with a different bank, such that the proceeds of the new loan are utilised to settle all or part of the old overdraft balance, a cash inflow and outflow have taken place. Consequently, the new loan would be shown in financing with the result that the net movement in the overdraft balance will automatically be reflected in the increase or decrease in cash for the period.

Cash subject to restriction

11.13 The treatment of cash subject to restriction in the cash flow statement is not specifically covered by the standard, although disclosure is required, where access is severely restricted (see para 10.11). Nevertheless, the question arises as to how they should be dealt with in the cash flow statement itself. Consider the following example.

Example

A property company has secured development finance of £10m from its bankers during the year ended 31 December 19X5. The funds are held in a special blocked account to be used only for a specific development. Development on the property commenced during the year and by the end of its financial year the company had expended £2m. At 31 December 19X5, there was a balance of £8m in the blocked account.

- There is a view that the balance of £8m in the blocked account should not be included in cash, because to do so would create a distorted impression of the company's liquidity position. In that situation, the company would show the net cash outflow of £2m from operating activities, a cash inflow of £10m in financing with the balance of £8m as fixed deposits under capital expenditure and financial investment. Adequate disclosure on the restrictions should also be given in a note if funds can only be drawn down with the banker's permission.

- An alternative treatment might be to treat the £8m balance as part of cash with a clear explanation of the nature of the restriction given either on the face of the cash flow statement or in the note that analyses the changes in net debt with balance sheet amounts.

The first presentation is correct because the definition of cash is not met in the second presentation. Cash held in a special blocked deposit account does not meet the narrow definition of cash as set out in the standard (see para 4.2).

11.14 In general, the treatment of cash subject to restriction should depend on the nature of the item and the restriction in force. For example, client money is not generally available for business's own use and falls outside the definition of cash, even though it may be reported in the balance sheet along with the related liability. Another situation is where a company is required to give a bond or a guarantee to a third party, for example, a bond may be held by Customs & Excise for the clearance of imported merchandise. In that situation, the payment to Customs would form part of operating cash flows. Where there are restrictions on the transfer of cash from a foreign subsidiary to the parent in the UK because of exchange control restrictions, the cash balances held in the foreign subsidiary would be treated as part of group cash in the cash flow statement, provided they meet the definition of cash in the foreign subsidiary that owns them. Furthermore, this restriction would need to be disclosed as stated in paragraph 10.11.

Chapter 12

Worked example

Introduction

12.1   A worked example showing how a cash flow statement would be prepared for a group in accordance with the standard is given below. In order to prepare a consolidated cash flow statement for Alphabeta Plc, the consolidated profit and loss account, the consolidated balance sheet and certain other information related to the company are given. The starting point in the preparation of a cash flow statement is to compute all the increases and decreases in balance sheet amounts between the current period and the preceding period. Once the increases and decreases have been identified, each one must be analysed to determine its effect, if any, on the net cash provided or used in operating activities, returns on investments and servicing of finance, taxation, capital expenditure and financial investment, acquisitions and disposals, equity dividends paid and financing. If any increase or decrease affects more than one of the standard headings, each one must be separately analysed. In the example, each figure in the cash flow statement can be traced to the profit and loss account or balance sheet (via workings) by following the note references shown on the cash flow statement. The example does not deal with foreign currency operations as they have been covered in an earlier example (see para 9.18). Comparative figures for the cash flow statement have not been presented. The presentation of the cash flow statement and the related notes follow the illustrative example given in the standard.

Illustration

Summarised below is the consolidated profit and loss account of Alphabeta Plc for the year ended 31 December 19X5, together with the consolidated balance sheets as at 31 December 19X5 and 19X4. A cash flow statement for the group for the year ended 31 December 19X5 including notes to that statement is also given. The detailed workings supporting the figures in the cash flow statement follow immediately after the notes.

Alphabeta Plc
Consolidated profit and loss account for the year ended 31 December 19X5

	£'000
Turnover	47,852
Cost of sales	35,889
Gross profit	11,963
Distribution costs	2,814
Administrative expenses	5,250
	3,899
Income from interests in associated company	230
Operating profit	4,129
Investment income	126
Interest payable and similar charges	(465)
Profit on ordinary activities before taxation	3,790
Taxation	1,600
Profit on ordinary activities after taxation	2,190
Minority interest	425
Profit for the financial year	1,765
Dividends	800
Retained profit for the year	965

Alphabeta Plc
Consolidated balance sheets

		19X5 £'000	19X4 £'000
Fixed assets			
Intangible assets	1	398	200
Tangible assets	2	17,082	12,800
Investments	6	1,230	833
		18,710	13,833
Current assets			
Stocks	3	6,586	6,821
Debtors	4	7,975	4,790
Investments		166	197
Cash at bank and in hand		2,541	2,050
		17,268	13,858
Creditors: amounts falling due within one year	5	10,909	8,085
Net current assets		6,359	5,773
Total assets less current liabilities		25,069	19,606

Creditors: amounts falling due after more than one year			
Debenture and other long-term loans	9	1,200	650
Obligations under finance leases	5	614	676
Provisions for liabilities and charges			
Pensions	10	426	103
Deferred tax	5	1,182	725
		3,422	2,154
Net assets		21,647	17,452
Capital and reserves			
Called up share capital	8	13,800	12,000
Share premium account	8	1,525	600
Revaluation reserve		600	392
Profit and loss account		4,225	3,260
Shareholders' funds		20,150	16,252
Minority interests	7	1,497	1,200
		21,647	17,452

Alphabeta Plc
Consolidated cash flow statement for the year ended 31 December 19X5

	Note	£'000	£'000
Net cash flow from operating activities	I		4,979
Returns on investments and servicing of finance	II		(507)
Taxation	5d		(879)
Capital expenditure and financial investment	II		(3,888)
Acquisitions and disposals	II		(115)
Equity dividends paid	5j		(700)
Cash outflow before management of liquid resources and financing			(1,110)

Management of liquid resources	II		(439)
Financing	II		
Issue of ordinary shares		925	
Increase in debt		<u>331</u>	1,256
Decrease in cash in the period			<u>(293)</u>

Reconciliation of net cash flow to movement in net debt (note III)		
	£'000	£'000
Decrease in cash in the period	(293)	
Cash outflow from increase in liquid resources	439	
Cash inflow from increase in debt and lease financing	<u>(331)</u>	
Change in net debt resulting from cash flows		(185)
New finance lease		<u>(228)</u>
Movement in net debt in the period		(413)
Net funds at 1 January 19X5		<u>47</u>
Net debt at 31 December 19X5		<u>(366)</u>

Notes to the cash flow statement

I Net cash flow from operating activities

		£'000	£'000
Operating profit			4,129
Amortisation of intangible fixed assets	1b		152
Depreciation on tangible fixed assets	2a		1,345
Gain on sale of tangible fixed assets	2c		(45)
Share of associated company's profits		(230)	
Less: dividends received	6b	150	(80)
Decrease in stocks	3a		600
Increase in trade debtors	4a		(2,432)
Increase in prepayments and accrued income	4b		(249)
Increase in trade creditors	5b		996
Decrease in amounts owed to associated company	5c		(50)
Increase in other taxation and social security	5e		254
Increase in accruals	5f		36
Increase in pension provisions	10a		323
Net cash flow from operating activities			4,979

II Analysis of cash flows for headings netted in the cash flow statement

		£'000
Returns on investments and servicing of finance		
Interest received	4c	102
Interest paid	5g	(236)
Interest element of finance lease rentals	5h	(120)
Premium paid on redemption of debentures	5i	(125)
Dividends paid to minorities	7a	(128)
Net cash outflow for returns on investments and servicing of finance		(507)
Capital expenditure and financial investment		
Purchase of patents	1a	(40)
Purchase of tangible fixed assets	2b	(3,974)
Sale of tangible fixed assets	2d	503
Purchase of fixed asset investments	6a	(377)
Net cash outflow for capital expenditure		(3,888)
Acquisitions and disposals	Note IV	
Purchase of subsidiary undertaking		(175)
Cash acquired with subsidiary		60
Net cash outflow for acquisitions and disposals		(115)

105

Management of liquid resources*	Note III	
Cash placed on short-term deposit		(470)
Sale of government securities		31
Net cash outflow from management of liquid resources		(439)

Financing

Issue of ordinary shares	8b	1,000
Expenses paid in connection with share issue	8a	(75)
Issue of shares		925
New secured loans	9a	750
Repayment of debentures	9b	(200)
Principal payment under finance lease	5a	(219)
Increase in debt		331
Net cash inflow from financing		1,256

* Alphabeta Plc includes term deposits and government securities held as current asset investments as liquid resources.

III Analysis of net debt

	1 Jan 19X5	Cash flow	Other non-cash changes	31 Dec 19X5
	£'000	£'000	£'000	£'000
Net cash:				
Cash at bank and in hand:	2,050			2,541
Less: deposits treated as liquid resources	(780)			(1,250)
	1,270	21		1,291
Bank overdraft	(700)	(314)		(1,014)
	570	(293)		277
Liquid resources:				
Deposits included in cash	780	470		1,250
Current asset investments	197	(31)		166
	977	439		1,416
Debt:				
Finance leases	(850)	219	(228)	(859)
Debts falling due after one year	(650)	(550)	-	(1,200)
	(1500)	(331)	(228)	(2,059)
Net debt	47	(185)	(228)	(366)

Analysed in Balance Sheet

Cash at bank and in hand	2,050	2,541
Current asset investments	197	166
Bank overdraft	(700)	(1,014)
Finance leases		
within one year	(174)	(245)
after one year	(676)	(614)
Debentures and other long-term loans		
after one year	(650)	(1,200)
	47	(366)

IV Acquisition of Zeta Limited

On 1 March 19X5, a new wholly subsidiary, Zeta Limited, was acquired by the issue of 1,200,000 ordinary shares of £1 each, whose fair market value was deemed to be £1.50 per share and £175,000 in cash. The fair values of Zeta Limited's identifiable assets and liabilities at the date of acquisition (including goodwill) were as follows:

Net assets acquired	**£'000**
Goodwill	310
Fixed assets	1,550
Stocks	365
Debtors	480
Cash at bank and in hand	60
Trade creditors	(655)
Accruals	(135)
	1,975
Satisfied by	
Shares allotted	1,800
Cash	175
	1,975

Zeta Limited contributed £482,000 to the group's net operating cash flows, paid £75,000 in respect of net returns on investments and servicing of finance, paid £127,000 in respect of taxation and utilised £250,000 for capital expenditure.

V   Major non-cash transactions

(a)   During the year the group entered into a finance lease arrangement in respect of equipment with a capital value at the inception of the lease of £228,000.

(b)   Part of the consideration for the purchase of Zeta Limited comprised shares. Further details of the acquisition are set out in note 4.

Cash flow statement workings

1   Analysis of intangible fixed assets

		£'000	£'000
Net book value at 31 December 19X4			
Net book value of patents and trade marks		50	
Goodwill net of amortisation		150	200
Additions during the year			
Patents and trade marks	a	40	
Goodwill arising on Zeta Ltd		310	350
Amortisation for the year			
On patents		10	
On goodwill	b	142	(152)
Net book value at 31 December 19X5			398

2   Analysis of tangible fixed assets

		£'000	£'000
Net book value at 31 December 19X4			12,800
Addition in respect of new subsidiary			1,550
Additions			4,327
Surplus on revaluations			208
Net book value of disposals			(458)
Depreciation for the year	a		(1,345)
Net book value at 31 December 19X5			17,082

Additions during the year include a warehouse constructed by the group for £1,925,000 of which £125,000 related to interest capitalised and new equipment purchased on a finance lease with a fair value of £228,000. Included in administrative expenses is £45,000 for the gain arising on sale of fixed assets.

Additions as above		4,327
Less: leased assets		(228)
Less: capitalised interest (see workings note 5)		(125)
Cash paid	b	3,974
Net book value of disposals		458
Gain arising on sale	c	45
Proceeds of sale	d	503

---

3 Stocks

		£'000
At 31 December 19X5		6,586
At 31 December 19X4		(6,821)
Decrease		(235)
Less: arising from acquisition of Zeta Ltd		(365)
Net decrease included in reconciliation (note 1)	a	(600)

---

4 Analysis of debtors

	19X5	19X4
	£'000	£'000
Trade debtors	7,327	4,415
Prepayments and accrued income	648	375
	7,975	4,790

Trade debtors are stated net of provisions for bad debts of £960,000 in 19X5 and £485,000 in 19X4 respectively. The group wrote off £175,000 in bad debts and recognised an additional provision of £650,000 in administrative expenses.

Trade debtors		£'000
Trade debtors at 31 December 19X5		7,327
Trade debtors at 31 December 19X4		(4,415)
Increase		2,912
Less: arising on acquisition of Zeta Ltd		(480)
Net increase included in reconciliation (note 1)	a	2,432

Note: The provision of £650,000 arising in the year has been included in the net movement on trade debtors and not separately identified.

Prepayments and accrued income

Included in prepayments and accrued income is interest receivable of £47,000 and £23,000 for 19X5 and 19X4 respectively.

	£'000	£'000
At 31 December 19X5	648	
Less: interest receivable	(47)	601
Less:		
At 31 December 19X4	375	
Less: interest receivable	(23)	(352)
Net increase included in reconciliation (note 1) **b**		249

Interest received

		£'000
Receivable at 31 December 19X4		23
Investment income per P&L account		126
Receivable at 31 December 19X5		(47)
Cash received	**c**	102

---

5   Analysis of creditors

	19X5	19X4
	£'000	£'000
Bank loans and overdrafts	1,014	700
Obligations under finance leases	245	174
Trade creditors	6,004	4,353
Amounts owed to associated companies	193	243
Corporation tax	746	575
Advance corporation tax	267	234
Other taxation and social security	440	186
Accruals	1,200	920
Dividends payable	800	700
	10,909	8,085

Bank loans and overdrafts for 19X5 and 19X4 are all repayable on demand and included in cash.

Obligations under finance leases		£'000	£'000
Obligations at 31 December 19X4			
Less than one year		174	
More than one year		676	850
New capital lease			228
Obligations at 31 December 19X5			
Less than one year		245	
More than one year		614	(859)
Principal payment under finance leases	a		219

Trade creditors		£'000
At 31 December 19X5		6,004
At 31 December 19X4		(4,353)
Increase		1,651
Less: arising on acquisition of Zeta Ltd		(655)
Net increase included in reconciliation (note 1)	b	996

Amounts owed to associated company		£'000
At 31 December 19X5		193
At 31 December 19X4		(243)
Net decrease	c	(50)

Amounts owed to the associated company arise on trading activities

Taxation		£'000	£'000
Balance at 31 December 19X4			
Corporation tax		575	
ACT		234	
Deferred tax		725	1,534
Tax charged per accounts:			
UK Corporation tax		980	
Transfer to deferred tax		457	
Prior year underprovision		103	
		1,540	1,540
Associated company		60	
Tax charged in P&L account		1,600	
Balance at 31 December 19X5			
Corporation tax		746	
ACT		267	
Deferred tax		1,182	(2,195)
Tax paid	d		879

111

Other taxation and social security		**£'000**
At 31 December 19X5		440
At 31 December 19X4		(186)
Net increase included in reconciliation (note 1)	e	254

Accruals

Included in accruals at 31 December 19X5 and 19X4 is interest payable of £154,000 and £45,000 respectively.

		£'000	**£'000**
At 31 December 19X5		1,200	
Less: interest payable		(154)	1,046
Less:			
At 31 December 19X4		920	
Less: interest payable		(45)	(875)
Net increase			171
Less: arising on acquisition of Zeta Ltd			(135)
Net increase included in reconciliation (note 1)	f		36

Interest paid on loans and finance leases:		**£'000**	**£'000**
Interest accrued at 31 December 19X4			45
Charge per P&L account:			
On overdrafts, bank and other loans		220	
On finance leases		120	
On premium paid on debenture redemption		125	465
Interest capitalised (see workings note 2)			125
Interest accrued at 31 December 19X5			(154)
Cash paid			481
Interest paid on overdrafts, bank & other loans	g		236
Interest paid on finance leases	h		120
Premium paid on debenture redemption	i		125
			481

Dividends paid by holding company		**£'000**
Balance at 31 December 19X4		700
Per P&L account		800
Balance at 31 December 19X5		(800)
Cash paid	j	700

6 Investments

		Associated company	Listed Investments	Total
		£'000	£'000	£'000
Balance at 31 December 19X4		603	230	833
Share of retained profits		20	-	20
Additions	a	-	377	377
Balance at 31 December 19X5		623	607	1,230
Share of associated company's profits (£230) less tax (£60)		170		
Less profits retained		20		
Dividends received	b	150		

Current asset investments

Current assets investments, which relate to British Government Securities, are classified as liquid resources by the group.

7 Minority interests

		£'000
Balance at 31 December 19X4		1,200
Profit for the year		425
Balance at 31 December 19X5		(1,497)
Dividends paid to minority shareholders	a	128

8 Share capital and share premium

		£'000	£'000
At 31 December 19X5			
Share capital		13,800	
Share premium		1,525	15,325
At 31 December 19X4			
Share capital		12,000	
Share premium		600	(12,600)
Net increase			2,725
Less: issued for purchase of Zeta Ltd			(1,800)
Add: share issue expenses written off	a		75
Balance issued for cash	b		1,000

9	Debentures and other loans		£'000
	At 31 December 19X5		1,200
	At 31 December 19X4		(650)
	Net increase		550
	Increase consists of:		
	New secured loans	a	750
	Repayment of debentures (nominal value)	b	(200)
			550

10	Provisions for liabilities and charges		
			£'000
	Pensions		
	At 31 December 19X5		426
	At 31 December 19X4		(103)
	Increase included in reconciliation (note 1)	a	323

Chapter 13

Comparison with IASs

13.1   The IASC rules are to be found in IAS 7, 'Cash flow statements', which was revised in 1992. These rules are significantly different from those included in the revised FRS 1. The principal differences, which are dealt with in appendix II to the standard, are summarised below:

- IAS 7 has none of the exemptions that allow many enterprises not to prepare cash flow statements under FRS 1.

- IAS 7 requires cash flows to be reported under three sections: operating, investing and financing, whereas FRS 1 requires cash flows to be reported in far greater detail under eight standard headings.

- The cash flows to be reported under IAS 7 relate to movements in cash and cash equivalents (defined as short-term highly liquid investments that are readily convertible into known amounts of cash and subject to insignificant risk of changes in value). The revised FRS 1 has dropped the notion of cash equivalents and requires the movement of cash (defined as cash in hand and deposits repayable on demand, less overdrafts) to be reported in the cash flow statement. Cash flows relating to former cash equivalents are reported under a new heading 'management of liquid resources'.

- IAS 7 requires most cash flows to be shown gross, whereas FRS 1 allows operating cash flows to be reported net or gross. [IAS 7 para 21]. IAS 7 requires net reporting of cash flows relating to customers where the cash flows reflect the activities of the customer rather than those of the entity. There is no equivalent provisions in FRS 1.

- IAS 7 does not require a reconciliation of movements in cash flows to the movement in net debt.

13.2   In 1994, the International Organisation of Securities Commission (IOSCO) recommended IAS 7 for the preparation of cash flow statements for cross-border listings. This has been followed by official endorsement of this by the SEC for filing of financial statements in the US by foreign registrants. This is the first (and, at the time of writing, the only) full IAS to be accepted in this way.

(REVISED 1996)

CASH FLOW

STATEMENTS

ACCOUNTING
STANDARDS
BOARD

Financial Reporting Standard 1 (Revised 1996) is set out in paragraphs 1-50.

The Statement of Standard Accounting Practice set out in paragraphs 4-50 should be read in the context of the Objective as stated in paragraph 1 and the definitions set out in paragraphs 2 and 3 and also of the Foreword to Accounting Standards and the Statement of Principles for Financial Reporting currently in issue.

The Explanation set out in paragraphs 51-68 shall be regarded as part of the Statement of Standard Accounting Practice insofar as it assists in interpreting that statement.

Appendix III 'The development of the FRS' reviews considerations and arguments that were thought significant by members of the Board in reaching the conclusions on FRS 1 (Revised 1996).

©The Accounting Standards Board Limited 1996
ISBN 1 85712 048 5

CONTENTS

ADOPTION OF FRS 1 (REVISED 1996) BY THE BOARD

APPENDICES

I EXAMPLES OF CASH FLOW STATEMENTS - for an individual company, a group, a bank and an insurance group

II COMPLIANCE WITH INTERNATIONAL ACCOUNTING STANDARDS

III THE DEVELOPMENT OF THE FRS

SUMMARY

General

a Financial Reporting Standard 1 (Revised 1996) 'Cash Flow Statements' requires reporting entities within its scope to prepare a cash flow statement in the manner set out in the FRS. Cash flows are increases or decreases in amounts of cash, and cash is cash in hand and deposits repayable on demand at any qualifying institution less overdrafts from any qualifying institution repayable on demand.

Scope

b The FRS applies to all financial statements intended to give a true and fair view of the financial position and profit or loss (or income and expenditure) except those of:

(i) subsidiary undertakings where 90 per cent or more of the voting rights are controlled within the group, provided that consolidated financial statements in which those subsidiary undertakings are included are publicly available;

(ii) mutual life assurance companies;

(iii) pension funds;

(iv) open-ended investment funds, subject to certain further conditions;

(v) for two years from the effective date of the FRS, building societies that, as required by law, prepare a statement of source and application of funds in a prescribed format; and

(vi) small entities (based on the small companies exemption in companies legislation).

Format for the cash flow statement

c   An entity's cash flow statement should list its cash flows for the period classified under the following standard headings:

- operating activities (using either the direct or indirect method)
- returns on investments and servicing of finance
- taxation
- capital expenditure and financial investment
- acquisitions and disposals
- equity dividends paid
- management of liquid resources
- financing.

The last two headings can be shown in a single section provided a subtotal is given for each heading.

d   Individual categories of inflows and outflows under the standard headings should be disclosed separately either in the cash flow statement or in a note to it unless they are allowed to be shown net. Cash inflows and outflows may be shown net if they relate to the management of liquid resources or financing and the inflows and outflows either:

(i)   relate in substance to a single financing transaction (which is one that fulfils the conditions in paragraph 35 of FRS 4 'Capital Instruments'*); or

---

* *The conditions set out in paragraph 35 of FRS 4 are:*

(a) *the debt and the facility are under a single agreement or course of dealing with the same lender or group of lenders;*

(b) *the finance costs for the new debt are on a basis that is not significantly higher than that of the existing debt;*

(c) *the obligations of the lender (or group of lenders) are firm: the lender is not able legally to refrain from providing funds except in circumstances the possibility of which can be demonstrated to be remote; and*

(d) *the lender (or group of lenders) is expected to be able to fulfil its obligations under the facility.*

(ii) are due to short maturities and high turnover occurring from rollover or reissue (for example, short-term deposits or a commercial paper programme).

The requirement to show cash inflows and outflows separately does not apply to cash flows relating to operating activities.

Links to other primary statements

e   Because the information given by a cash flow statement is best appreciated in the context of the information given by the other primary statements, the FRS requires two reconciliations, between:

(i) operating profit and the net cash flow from operating activities; and

(ii) the movement in cash in the period and the movement in net debt.

Neither reconciliation forms part of the cash flow statement but each may be given either adjoining the statement or in a separate note.

f   The movement in net debt should identify the following components and reconcile these to the opening and closing balance sheet amounts:

- the cash flows of the entity
- the acquisition or disposal of subsidiary undertakings (excluding cash balances)
- other non-cash changes
- the recognition of changes in market value and exchange rate movements.

Insurance companies and groups

g   Insurance companies and groups should include the cash flows of their long-term business only to the extent of cash transferred to, and available to meet the obligations of, the company or group as a whole. The cash flow statement of an insurance company or group should include a section for cash flows relating to portfolio investments rather than a section for cash flows relating to the management of liquid resources.

Banks

h   The cash flow statement of an entity qualifying as a bank should include under operating activities cash flows relating to investments held for trading. A bank need not include a section on the management of liquid resources or the reconciliation of cash flows to the movement in net debt.

Other disclosures

i   Material transactions not resulting in movements of cash should be disclosed in the notes to the cash flow statement, if the disclosure is necessary for an understanding of the underlying transactions. A consolidated cash flow statement should identify and explain the circumstances and effect of restrictions preventing the transfer of cash from one part of the group to meet obligations of another.

FINANCIAL REPORTING STANDARD 1 (Revised 1996)

OBJECTIVE

1   The objective of this FRS is to ensure that reporting entities falling within its scope:

(a) report their cash generation and cash absorption for a period by highlighting the significant components of cash flow in a way that facilitates comparison of the cash flow performance of different businesses; and

(b) provide information that assists in the assessment of their liquidity, solvency and financial adaptability.

DEFINITIONS

2   The following definitions shall apply in this FRS and in
particular in the Statement of Standard Accounting
Practice set out in paragraphs 4-50.

Active market:-
A market of sufficient depth to absorb the investment held
without a significant effect on the price.

Bank:-
An entity whose business is to receive deposits or other
repayable funds from the public and to grant credits for its
own account.*

Cash:-
Cash in hand and deposits repayable on demand with any
qualifying financial institution, less overdrafts from any
qualifying financial institution repayable on demand.
Deposits are repayable on demand if they can be
withdrawn at any time without notice and without penalty
or if a maturity or period of notice of not more than 24
hours or one working day has been agreed. Cash includes
cash in hand and deposits denominated in foreign
currencies.

Cash flow:-
An increase or decrease in an amount of cash.

Equity dividends:-
Dividends relating to equity shares as defined in paragraph
7 of FRS 4 'Capital Instruments'.

---

* *This definition is based on:*

(a) *in Great Britain, section 262 of the Companies Act 1985, itself based on the definition
in the Banking Act 1987;*

(b) *in Northern Ireland, Article 270 of the Companies (Northern Ireland) Order 1986;*

(c) *in the Republic of Ireland, section 2(2) (other than paragraph (b)) of the Companies
(Amendment) Act 1986.*

Insurance company or group:-

A company that carries on insurance business and is regulated accordingly or an insurance group as defined in the relevant legislation.*

Investment fund:-†

An entity:

(a) whose business consists of investing its funds mainly in securities, with the aim of spreading investment risk and giving members the benefit of the results of the management of its funds;

(b) none of whose holdings in other entities (except those in other investment funds) represents more than 15 per cent by value of the investing entity's investments; and

(c) that has not retained more than 15 per cent of the income it derives from securities.

Liquid resources:-

Current asset investments held as readily disposable stores of value. A readily disposable investment is one that:

(a) is disposable by the reporting entity without curtailing or disrupting its business;

and is either:

(b)(i) readily convertible into known amounts of cash at or close to its carrying amount, or

(b)(ii) traded in an active market.

---

* *In the UK an insurance company is one to which Part II of the Insurance Companies Act 1982 applies. The equivalent reference in the Republic of Ireland is the Companies (Amendment) Act 1986 section 2(3). In the UK an insurance group is defined in section 255A(5) of the Companies Act 1985. In the Republic of Ireland an insurance company or group is one to which Regulation 3 of the European Community (Insurance Undertakings: Accounts) Regulations 1996 applies.*

† *This definition is based on three of the four conditions defining an investment company in companies legislation—in Great Britain section 266 of the Companies Act 1985; in Northern Ireland, Article 274 of the Companies (Northern Ireland) Order 1986; and in the Republic of Ireland, section 47 of the Companies (Amendment) Act 1983. Under the definition above, investment companies as defined in companies legislation will qualify as investment funds but so should certain investment entities that are not companies or do not qualify under companies legislation because they distribute capital.*

Net debt:-
The borrowings of the reporting entity (comprising debt as defined in FRS 4 'Capital Instruments' (paragraph 6), together with related derivatives, and obligations under finance leases) less cash and liquid resources. Where cash and liquid resources exceed the borrowings of the entity reference should be to 'net funds' rather than to 'net debt'.

Non-equity dividends:-
Dividends relating to non-equity shares as defined in paragraph 12 of FRS 4 'Capital Instruments'.

Overdraft:-
A borrowing facility repayable on demand that is used by drawing on a current account with a qualifying financial institution.

Qualifying financial institution:-
An entity that as part of its business receives deposits or other repayable funds and grants credits for its own account.

3   References to companies legislation mean:

(a) in Great Britain, the Companies Act 1985;

(b) in Northern Ireland, the Companies (Northern Ireland) Order 1986; and

(c) in the Republic of Ireland, the Companies Acts 1963-90 and the European Communities (Companies: Group Accounts) Regulations 1992.

STATEMENT OF STANDARD ACCOUNTING PRACTICE

4   Reporting entities falling within the scope of paragraph 5 of Financial Reporting Standard 1 (Revised 1996) are required to provide as a primary statement within the reporting entity's financial statements a cash flow statement drawn up in accordance with the standard accounting principles set out in paragraphs 6–48 of the FRS.

Scope

5   The FRS applies to all financial statements intended to give a true and fair view of the financial position and profit or loss (or income and expenditure) except those of:

(a) subsidiary undertakings where 90 per cent or more of the voting rights are controlled within the group, provided that consolidated financial statements in which the subsidiary undertakings are included are publicly available.

(b) mutual life assurance companies.

(c) pension funds.

(d) open-ended investment funds that meet all the following conditions:

    (i) substantially all of the entity's investments are highly liquid;

    (ii) substantially all of the entity's investments are carried at market value; and

    (iii) the entity provides a statement of changes in net assets.

(e) for two years from the effective date of the FRS, building societies, as defined by the Building Societies Act 1986 in the UK and by the Building Societies Act 1989 in the Republic of Ireland, that prepare, as required by law, a statement of source and application of funds in a prescribed format.

(f) companies incorporated under companies legislation and entitled to the exemptions available in the legislation for small companies when filing accounts with the Registrar of Companies.

(g) entities that would have been in category (f) above if they were companies incorporated under companies legislation.

Preparation of cash flow statements

6   The cash flow statement should include all the reporting entity's inflows and outflows of cash. Transactions that do not result in cash flows of the reporting entity should not be reported in the cash flow statement.

Format for cash flow statements

7   An entity's cash flow statement should list its cash flows for the period classified under the following standard headings:

- operating activities
- returns on investments and servicing of finance
- taxation
- capital expenditure and financial investment
- acquisitions and disposals
- equity dividends paid
- management of liquid resources
- financing.

The first six headings should be in the sequence set out above. Operating cash flows can be presented by either the direct method (showing the relevant constituent cash flows) or the indirect method (calculating operating cash flows by adjustment to the operating profit reported in the profit and loss account). The cash flows relating to the management of liquid resources and financing can be combined under a single heading provided that the cash flows relating to each are shown separately and separate subtotals are given. Appendix I of the FRS contains examples of cash flow statements for an individual company, a group, a bank and an insurance group.

Classification of cash flows

8   Except for cash inflows and outflows that are shown net (as permitted by paragraph 9), the individual categories of inflows and outflows under the standard headings set out in paragraphs 11–32 should be disclosed separately, where material, in the cash flow statement or in a note. The cash flow classifications may be subdivided further to give a fuller description of the activities of the reporting entity or to provide segmental information.

9   The requirement to show cash inflows and outflows separately does not apply to cash flows relating to operating activities. Cash inflows and outflows within the management of liquid resources or financing may also be netted against each other if they either:

(a) relate in substance to a single financing transaction (which is one that fulfils the conditions in paragraph 35 of FRS 4 'Capital Instruments'*); or

(b) are due to short maturities and high turnover occurring from rollover or reissue (for example, short-term deposits or a commercial paper programme).

10 Each cash flow should be classified according to the substance of the transaction giving rise to it. That substance should be used to determine the most appropriate standard heading under which to report any cash flows that are not specified in the categories set out in paragraphs 11-32 below. However, cash flows relating to interest paid should always be classified under 'returns on investments and servicing of finance' even if the interest has been capitalised in the other primary statements.

---

* *The conditions set out in paragraph 35 of FRS 4 are:*

(a) the debt and the facility are under a single agreement or course of dealing with the same lender or group of lenders;

(b) the finance costs for the new debt are on a basis that is not significantly higher than that of the existing debt;

(c) the obligations of the lender (or group of lenders) are firm: the lender is not able legally to refrain from providing funds except in circumstances the possibility of which can be demonstrated to be remote; and

(d) the lender (or group of lenders) is expected to be able to fulfil its obligations under the facility.

Classification of cash flows by standard heading

Operating activities

11 Cash flows from operating activities are in general the cash effects of transactions and other events relating to operating or trading activities, normally shown in the profit and loss account in arriving at operating profit. They include cash flows in respect of operating items relating to provisions, whether or not the provision was included in operating profit. Dividends received from equity accounted entities should be included as operating cash flows where the results are included as part of operating profit.

12 A reconciliation between the operating profit reported in the profit and loss account and the net cash flow from operating activities should be given either adjoining the cash flow statement or as a note. The reconciliation is not part of the cash flow statement: if adjoining the cash flow statement, it should be clearly labelled and kept separate. The reconciliation should disclose separately the movements in stocks, debtors and creditors related to operating activities and other differences between cash flows and profits. The reconciliation should also show separately the difference between dividends received and results taken into account for equity accounted entities.

Returns on investments and servicing of finance

13 'Returns on investments and servicing of finance' are receipts resulting from the ownership of an investment and payments to providers of finance, non-equity shareholders (eg the holders of preference shares) and minority interests, excluding those items required by paragraphs 11-32 to be classified under another heading.

14 Cash inflows from returns on investments and servicing of finance include:

    (a) interest received, including any related tax recovered; and

    (b) dividends received, net of any tax credits (except dividends from equity accounted entities whose results are included as part of operating profit).

15 Cash outflows from returns on investments and servicing of finance include:

    (a) interest paid (even if capitalised), including any tax deducted and paid to the relevant tax authority;

    (b) cash flows that are treated as finance costs under FRS 4 (this will include issue costs on debt and non-equity share capital);

    (c) the interest element of finance lease rental payments;

    (d) dividends paid on non-equity shares of the entity; and

    (e) dividends paid to minority interests.

Taxation

16 The cash flows included under the heading 'taxation' are cash flows to or from taxation authorities in respect of the reporting entity's revenue and capital profits. For a subsidiary undertaking, cash flows relating to group relief should be included in this section. Cash flows in respect of other taxation, including payments and receipts in respect of Value Added Tax, other sales taxes, property taxes and other taxes not assessed on the profits of the reporting entity, should be dealt with as set out in paragraphs 39-40 of the FRS.

17 Taxation cash inflows include cash receipts from the relevant tax authority of tax rebates, claims or returns of overpayments. For a subsidiary undertaking, payments received from other members of the group for group relief should be included as cash inflows.

18 Taxation cash outflows include cash payments to the relevant tax authority of tax, including payments of advance corporation tax. For a subsidiary undertaking, payments made to other members of the group for group relief should be included as cash outflows.

Capital expenditure and financial investment

19 The cash flows included in 'capital expenditure and financial investment' are those related to the acquisition or disposal of any fixed asset other than one required to be classified under 'acquisitions and disposals' as specified in paragraphs 22-24 of the FRS and any current asset investment not included in liquid resources dealt with in paragraphs 26-28. If no cash flows relating to financial investment fall to be included under this heading the caption may be reduced to 'capital expenditure'.

20 Cash inflows from 'capital expenditure and financial investment' include:

(a) receipts from sales or disposals of property, plant or equipment; and

(b) receipts from the repayment of the reporting entity's loans to other entities or sales of debt instruments of other entities other than receipts forming part of an acquisition or disposal or a movement in liquid resources, as specified respectively in paragraphs 22-24 and 26-28 of the FRS.

21 Cash outflows from 'capital expenditure and financial investment' include:

(a) payments to acquire property, plant or equipment; and

(b) loans made by the reporting entity and payments to acquire debt instruments of other entities other than payments forming part of an acquisition or disposal or a movement in liquid resources, as specified respectively in paragraphs 22-24 and 26-28 of the FRS.

Acquisitions and disposals

22 The cash flows included in 'acquisitions and disposals' are those related to the acquisition or disposal of any trade or business, or of an investment in an entity that is or, as a result of the transaction, becomes or ceases to be either an associate, a joint venture, or a subsidiary undertaking.

23 Cash inflows from 'acquisitions and disposals' include:

(a) receipts from sales of investments in subsidiary undertakings, showing separately any balances of cash and overdrafts transferred as part of the sale;

(b) receipts from sales of investments in associates or joint ventures; and

(c) receipts from sales of trades or businesses.

24 Cash outflows from 'acquisitions and disposals' include:

(a) payments to acquire investments in subsidiary undertakings, showing separately any balances of cash and overdrafts acquired;

(b) payments to acquire investments in associates and joint ventures; and

(c) payments to acquire trades or businesses.

Equity dividends paid

25 The cash outflows included in 'equity dividends paid' are dividends paid on the reporting entity's, or, in a group, the parent's, equity shares, excluding any advance corporation tax.

Management of liquid resources

26 The 'management of liquid resources' section should include cash flows in respect of liquid resources as defined in paragraph 2. Each entity should explain what it includes as liquid resources and any changes in its policy. The cash flows in this section can be shown in a single section with those under 'financing' provided that separate subtotals for each are given.

27 Cash inflows in management of liquid resources include:

(a) withdrawals from short-term deposits not qualifying as cash in so far as not netted under paragraph 9(b); and

(b) inflows from disposal or redemption of any other investments held as liquid resources.

28 Cash outflows in management of liquid resources include :

    (a) payments into short-term deposits not qualifying as cash in so far as not netted under paragraph 9(b); and

    (b) outflows to acquire any other investments held as liquid resources.

Financing

29 Financing cash flows comprise receipts or repayments of principal from or to external providers of finance. The cash flows in this section can be shown in a single section with those under 'management of liquid resources' provided that separate subtotals for each are given.

30 Financing cash inflows include:

    (a) receipts from issuing shares or other equity instruments; and

    (b) receipts from issuing debentures, loans, notes, and bonds and from other long-term and short-term borrowings (other than overdrafts).

31 Financing cash outflows include:

    (a) repayments of amounts borrowed (other than overdrafts);

    (b) the capital element of finance lease rental payments;

    (c) payments to reacquire or redeem the entity's shares; and

    (d) payments of expenses or commissions on any issue of equity shares.

32   The amounts of any financing cash flows received from or paid to equity accounted entities should be disclosed separately.

Reconciliation to net debt

33   A note reconciling the movement of cash in the period with the movement in net debt should be given either adjoining the cash flow statement or in a note.   The reconciliation is not part of the cash flow statement: if adjoining the cash flow statement, it should be clearly labelled and kept separate.   The changes in net debt should be analysed from the opening to the closing component amounts showing separately, where material, changes resulting from:

(a)   the cash flows of the entity;

(b)   the acquisition or disposal of subsidiary undertakings;

(c)   other non-cash changes; and

(d)   the recognition of changes in market value and exchange rate movements.

Where several balance sheet amounts or parts thereof have to be combined to form the components of opening and closing net debt, sufficient detail should be shown to enable the cash and other components of net debt to be respectively traced back to the amounts shown under the equivalent captions in the balance sheet.   A possible format for the analysis of net debt is provided in the examples in Appendix I.

Banks

34 Banks should include as cash only cash and balances at central banks and loans and advances to banks repayable on demand. The cash flow statement of a bank should include under operating activities receipts and payments relating to loans made to other entities and cash flows relating to investments held for trading. A bank need not include a section on the management of liquid resources nor the reconciliation of cash flows to the movement in net debt. Appendix I contains an example of a cash flow statement for a bank.

Insurance companies and groups

35 The cash flow statement of an entity qualifying as an insurance company or group should include a section for cash flows relating to 'portfolio investments' rather than a section for cash flows relating to the 'management of liquid resources'. Instead of the analysis of the movement in net debt that is generally required, insurance companies and groups should provide an analysis of the movement in portfolio investments less financing, either adjoining the cash flow statement or in a note. The reconciliation is not part of the cash flow statement: if adjoining the cash flow statement, it should be clearly labelled and kept separate. The reconciliation of operating profit to net cash flow from operating activities should normally take profit or loss on ordinary activities before tax as its starting point. Appendix I contains an example of a cash flow statement for an insurance group.

36 Insurance companies and groups, other than mutual life assurance companies to which the FRS does not apply, should include the cash flows of their long-term business—long-term life, pensions and annuity businesses or their equivalents in relation to overseas operations—only to the extent of cash transferred and available to meet the obligations of the company or group as a whole. The note analysing the movements in the balance sheet amounts of portfolio investments and financing during the period should distinguish movements relating to the long-term business to the extent that these are included in the balance sheet amounts.

Exceptional and extraordinary items and cash flows

37 Where cash flows relate to items that are classified as exceptional or extraordinary in the profit and loss account they should be shown under the appropriate standard headings, according to the nature of each item. The cash flows relating to exceptional or extraordinary items should be identified in the cash flow statement or a note to it and the relationship between the cash flows and the originating exceptional or extraordinary item should be explained.

38 Where cash flows are exceptional because of their size or incidence but are not related to items that are treated as exceptional or extraordinary in the profit and loss account, sufficient disclosure should be given to explain their cause and nature.

Value Added Tax and other taxes

39 Cash flows should be shown net of any attributable Value Added Tax or other sales tax unless the tax is irrecoverable by the reporting entity. The net movement on the amount payable to, or receivable from, the taxing authority should be allocated to cash flows from operating activities unless a different treatment is more appropriate in the particular circumstances concerned. Where restrictions apply to the recoverability of such taxes, the irrecoverable amount should be allocated to those expenditures affected by the restrictions. If this is impracticable, the irrecoverable tax should be included under the most appropriate standard heading.

40 Taxation cash flows other than those in respect of the reporting entity's revenue and capital profits and Value Added Tax, or other sales tax, should be included within the cash flow statement under the same standard heading as the cash flow that gave rise to the taxation cash flow, unless a different treatment is more appropriate in the particular circumstances concerned.

Foreign currencies

41 Where a portion of a reporting entity's business is undertaken by a foreign entity, the cash flows of that entity are to be included in the cash flow statement on the basis used for translating the results of those activities in the profit and loss account of the reporting entity. The same basis should be used in presenting the movements in stocks, debtors and creditors in the reconciliation between operating profit and cash from operating activities. Where intragroup cash flows are separately identifiable and the actual rate of exchange at which they took place is known, that rate, or an approximation thereto, may be used to translate the cash flows in order to ensure that they cancel on consolidation. If the rate used to translate intragroup cash flows is not the actual rate, any exchange rate differences arising should be included in the effect of exchange rate movements shown as part of the reconciliation to net debt.

Hedging transactions

42 When a futures contract, forward contract, option contract or swap contract is accounted for as a hedge, the cash flows of the contract should be reported under the same standard heading as the transaction that is the subject of the hedge.

Groups

43 Cash flows that are internal to the group should be eliminated in the preparation of a consolidated cash flow statement. Where a subsidiary undertaking joins or leaves a group during a financial year the cash flows of the group should include the cash flows of the subsidiary undertaking concerned for the same period as that for which the group's profit and loss account includes the results of the subsidiary undertaking.

44 The cash flows of any equity accounted entity should be included in the group cash flow statement only to the extent of the actual cash flows between the group and the entity concerned, for example dividends received in cash and loans made or repaid.

Acquisitions and disposals of subsidiary undertakings

45 A note to the cash flow statement should show a summary of the effects of acquisitions and disposals of subsidiary undertakings indicating how much of the consideration comprised cash. Material effects on amounts reported under each of the standard headings reflecting the cash flows of a subsidiary undertaking acquired or disposed of in the period should be disclosed, as far as practicable. This information could be given by dividing cash flows between continuing and discontinued operations and acquisitions.

Material non-cash transactions

46 Material transactions not resulting in movements of cash of the reporting entity should be disclosed in the notes to the cash flow statement if disclosure is necessary for an understanding of the underlying transactions.

Restrictions on remittability

47 A note to the cash flow statement should identify the amounts and explain the circumstances where restrictions prevent the transfer of cash from one part of the business or group to another.

Comparative figures

48 Comparative figures should be given for all items in the cash flow statement and such notes thereto as are required by the FRS with the exception of the note to the statement that analyses changes in the balance sheet amounts making up net debt (or the equivalent note for insurance companies and groups) and the note of the material effects of acquisitions and disposals of subsidiary undertakings on each of the standard headings.

Date from which effective

49 The accounting practices set out in the FRS should be regarded as standard in respect of financial statements relating to accounting periods ending on or after 23 March 1997. Earlier adoption is encouraged but not required.

Withdrawal of FRS 1 (issued September 1991)

50 The FRS supersedes FRS 1 issued in September 1991.

EXPLANATION

Definitions

Cash flows

51 Cash flows are defined as increases or decreases in cash. Cash includes cash in hand, deposits repayable on demand and overdrafts. Deposits are repayable on demand if they are in practice available within 24 hours without penalty. No investments, however liquid or near maturity, are included as cash. Overdrafts are included as cash because of their role as negative cash balances—a cheque drawn on an account can either reduce the cash balance or increase the overdraft. Although banks take large volumes of short-term and demand deposits, they do not usually have borrowings with the characteristics of an overdraft.

Liquid resources

52 The definition of liquid resources is expressed in general terms, emphasising the liquidity of the investment and its function as a readily disposable store of value rather than setting out a narrow range of investment instruments. Depending on the entity's policy (which should be disclosed), term deposits, government securities, loan stock, equities and derivatives may each form part of that entity's liquid resources, provided they meet the definition. Short-term deposits would also fall within the definition, though the requirement that they should be readily convertible into known amounts of cash at or close to their carrying amounts would tend to exclude any that are more than one year from maturity on acquisition.

Net debt

53 The objective of the reconciliation of cash flows to the movement in net debt is to provide information that assists in the assessment of liquidity, solvency and financial adaptability. Net debt is defined to include borrowings less liquid resources because movements in net debt so defined are widely used as indicating changes in liquidity, and therefore assist in assessing the financial strength of the entity. The definition excludes non-equity shares of the entity because, although these have features that may be similar to those of borrowings, they are not actually liabilities of the entity. The definition also excludes debtors and creditors because, while these are short-term claims on and sources of finance to the entity, their main role is as part of the entity's trading activities.

Scope

54 Most small reporting entities are exempt from the requirement to include a cash flow statement as part of their financial statements. This exemption does not extend to public companies or to banking companies, insurance companies, authorised persons under the Financial Services Act 1986,* or members of a group containing one or more of the above-mentioned entities. The scope of this exemption is currently being re-examined as part of a wider examination of the reporting requirements for small entities. However, the Board encourages small reporting entities to include a cash flow statement as part of their financial statements, if it would provide useful information to users of those financial statements and the benefits of the exercise outweigh the costs.

---

* *In the UK. The equivalent reference in the Republic of Ireland is the Investment Intermediaries Act 1995.*

Classification of cash flows

55 In setting the conditions for netting cash flows, paragraph 9 permits the cash flows over the period of a single financing transaction to be reported net. A single financing transaction is one that fulfils the conditions in paragraph 35 of FRS 4 'Capital Instruments' that determine when committed facilities can be taken into account in determining the maturity of debt.

56 In order to improve the comparability of cash flow statements of different entities, paragraphs 11-31 give examples of certain standard subdivisions that should be separately disclosed, if material. Reporting entities are encouraged, however, to disclose additional information relevant to their particular circumstances. One form of segmentation that may often be useful is a division of cash flows from operating activities into those relating to continuing and to discontinued operations (as defined in FRS 3 'Reporting Financial Performance'). In some circumstances it may also be useful to divide cash flows in a way that reflects different degrees of access to the underlying cash balances—this may be of especial relevance in regulated industries such as the insurance industry.

57 Certain accounting standards, such as SSAP 13 'Accounting for research and development', SSAP 21 'Accounting for leases and hire purchase contracts', FRS 4 'Capital Instruments' and FRS 5 'Reporting the Substance of Transactions', specify how certain transactions are to be recognised and classified for financial reporting on the basis of the substance of the transaction. In order to achieve consistent treatment in the cash flow statement this FRS requires cash flows, too, to be classified according to the substance of the transaction giving rise to them. For example, cash flows relating to development costs that are capitalised would be included under 'capital expenditure'. Cash flows relating to finance leases are to be divided into the part relating to interest, to be classified under 'servicing

of finance', and the part making up repayment of the capital amount, to be classified under 'financing'. Similarly, the cash flows relating to finance costs, as calculated by applying FRS 4, are to be classified under 'returns on investments and servicing of finance'. However, the Board believes that it is important to show the total of cash flows relating to interest paid in the cash flow statement. The FRS therefore requires interest paid to be included as servicing of finance, regardless of whether it is capitalised.

Classification of cash flows by standard heading

Operating activities

58 The FRS allows operating cash flows to be presented using either the direct or the indirect method. A cash flow statement presented under the direct method shows operating cash receipts and payments (including, in particular, cash receipts from customers, cash payments to suppliers and cash payments to and on behalf of employees), aggregating to the net cash flow from operating activities. Rather than reporting the individual component cash flows to arrive at the net cash inflow or outflow from operating activities, the cash flow statement under the indirect method derives the net cash inflow or outflow by means of a reconciliation from operating profit. The FRS requires the reconciliation even if the direct method is used. The reconciliation adjusts operating profit for non-cash charges and credits and brings in operating item cash flows relating to provisions, whether or not the provision was deducted in arriving at operating profit. Examples of such cash flows are redundancy payments falling under a provision for the termination of an operation or for a fundamental reorganisation or restructuring (paragraph 20a and b of FRS 3 'Reporting Financial Performance'), also operating item cash flows provided for on an acquisition.

59 In some businesses material debtors and creditors may arise in relation to the purchase and sale of investments, including investments forming part of liquid resources. The changes in such debtors and creditors should be included in the reconciliation of operating profit to the net cash flow from operating activities only to the extent that the purchase and sale of the investments giving rise to them form part of the operating activities of the entity.

Returns on investments and servicing of finance

60 Interest paid and received and dividends received may result from investing activities, the management of liquid resources, financing or in some cases operating activities. To the extent that entities such as banks, insurance companies or investment companies show interest received or paid and dividends received in their profit and loss accounts as part of their operating profit they should include related cash flows as part of their operating cash flows, unless the interest paid clearly relates to financing— for example, relating to a bank's subordinated loans—in which case it should be included under 'returns on investments and servicing of finance'.

Taxation

61 The taxation cash flows of a reporting entity in relation to revenue and capital profits may result from complex computations that are affected by the operating, investing and financing activities of an entity. The Board believes that it is not useful to divide taxation cash flows into constituent parts relating to the activities that gave rise to them because the apportionment will, in many cases, have to be made on an arbitrary basis. As taxation cash flows generally arise from activities in an earlier period, apportioning the taxation cash flows would in any event not necessarily report the taxation cash flows along with the transactions that gave rise to them. Accordingly, the Board believes that taxation cash flows in relation to revenue and capital profits should be disclosed in a separate section within the cash flow statement entitled 'taxation'.

Insurance companies and groups

62 One purpose of a cash flow statement is to provide information that assists in the assessment of the liquidity, solvency and financial adaptability of an entity. This objective, however, is of only limited application to an insurance company or group. In interpreting the information given by the cash flow statement of an insurance company or group, users should bear in mind that cash inflows of premiums to insurance companies may not increase their liquidity in the same way as cash received for interest or dividends because the receipt of premiums engenders provision requirements for future claims and reserve requirements for solvency.

Exceptional and extraordinary items and cash flows

63 The FRS requires cash flows relating to exceptional or extraordinary items to be identified and explained, to allow a user to gain an understanding of the effect of the underlying transactions on the cash flows. This requirement means that cash flows relating to reorganisation charges that are exceptional must be disclosed separately and explained. The FRS also requires identification of cash flows that are exceptional because of their size or incidence but are not related to items that are treated as exceptional or extraordinary in the profit and loss account. For a cash flow to be exceptional on the grounds of its size alone, it must be exceptional in relation to cash flows of a similar nature. A large prepayment against a pension liability is an example of a possible exceptional cash flow unrelated to an exceptional or extraordinary item in the profit and loss account.

Value Added Tax

64 The cash flows of an entity include Value Added Tax (VAT) where appropriate and thus strictly the various elements of the cash flow statement should include VAT. However, this treatment does not take into account the fact that normally VAT is a short-term timing difference as far as the entity's overall cash flows are concerned and the inclusion of VAT in the cash flows may distort the allocation of cash flows to standard headings. The Board believes that, in order to avoid this distortion and to show cash flows attributable to the reporting entity's activities, cash flows should be shown net of sales taxes and the net movement on the amount payable to, or receivable from, the taxing authority should be allocated to cash flows from operating activities unless a different treatment is more appropriate in the particular circumstances concerned.

Foreign currencies

65 Because of the complementary nature of the profit and loss account and the cash flow statement in reflecting different but related aspects of an entity's performance in the period, the standard requires the cash flow statement to be translated using the same rate as the profit and loss account, unless the actual rate at the date of the transaction is used. Cash flows between members of a group should not be included in the consolidated cash flow statement. However, these cash flows may not cancel unless the actual rate at the date of transfer is used for translation. The FRS allows the actual rate to be used where intragroup cash flows are separately identifiable and the actual rate is known.

Hedging transactions

66   Entities may undertake hedging transactions that result in cash flows. The Board is considering as part of its project on derivatives and other financial instruments the way in which such transactions should be reflected in financial statements. As an interim measure it has decided to confine the recognition of hedges in cash flow statements. An example of the presentation of a hedging transaction in accordance with the FRS would be the inclusion under 'returns on investments and servicing of finance' of the cash flows of interest rate swaps held as a hedge of an entity's own debt.

Material non-cash transactions

67   Consideration for transactions may be in a form other than cash. Since the purpose of a cash flow statement is to report cash flows, non-cash transactions should not be reported in a cash flow statement. However, to obtain a full picture of the alterations in financial position caused by the transactions for the period, separate disclosure of material non-cash transactions (such as shares issued for the acquisition of a subsidiary, the exchange of major assets or the inception of a finance lease contract) is also necessary.

Restrictions on remittability

68   The note identifying the amounts and explaining the circumstances where restrictions prevent the transfer of cash from one part of the business or group to another should refer only to circumstances where access is severely restricted by external factors such as strict exchange control rather than where the sole constraint is a special purpose designated by the reporting entity itself. Depending on the regulatory environment, cash balances in escrow, deposited with a regulator or held within an employee share ownership trust may be subject to restrictions on remittability that should be disclosed.

ADOPTION OF FRS 1 (REVISED 1996) BY THE BOARD

Financial Reporting Standard 1 (Revised 1996) - 'Cash Flow Statements' was approved for issue by the nine members of the Accounting Standards Board.

Sir David Tweedie   (Chairman)

Allan Cook   (Technical Director)

David Allvey

Ian Brindle

John Coombe

Raymond Hinton

Huw Jones

Professor Geoffrey Whittington

Ken Wild

CONTENTS OF APPENDICES

EXAMPLE 1 XYZ LIMITED
CASH FLOW STATEMENT FOR THE YEAR
ENDED 31 DECEMBER 1996

Reconciliation of operating profit to net cash inflow from operating activities

	£000	£000
Operating profit		6,022
Depreciation charges		899
Increase in stocks		(194)
Increase in debtors		(72)
Increase in creditors		234
Net cash inflow from operating activities		6,889

CASH FLOW STATEMENT

Net cash inflow from operating activities	6,889
Returns on investments and servicing of finance (note 1)	2,999
Taxation	(2,922)
Capital expenditure	(1,525)
	5,441
Equity dividends paid	(2,417)
	3,024
Management of liquid resources (note 1)	(450)
Financing (note 1)	57
Increase in cash	**2,631**

Reconciliation of net cash flow to movement in net debt (note 2)

Increase in cash in the period	2,631	
Cash to repurchase debenture	149	
Cash used to increase liquid resources	450	
Change in net debt*		3,230
Net debt at 1.1.96		(2,903)
Net funds at 31.12.96		327

---

* *In this example all changes in net debt are cash flows.*

NOTES TO THE CASH FLOW STATEMENT

Note 1 - GROSS CASH FLOWS

	£000	£000
Returns on investments and servicing of finance		
Interest received	3,011	
Interest paid	(12)	
		2,999
Capital expenditure		
Payments to acquire intangible fixed assets	(71)	
Payments to acquire tangible fixed assets	(1,496)	
Receipts from sales of tangible fixed assets	42	
		(1,525)
Management of liquid resources		
Purchase of treasury bills	(650)	
Sale of treasury bills	200	
		(450)
Financing		
Issue of ordinary share capital	211	
Repurchase of debenture loan	(149)	
Expenses paid in connection with share issues	(5)	
		57

Note 2 - ANALYSIS OF CHANGES IN NET DEBT

	At 1 Jan 1996 £000	Cash flows £000	Other changes £000	At 31 Dec 1996 £000
Cash in hand, at bank	42	847		889
Overdrafts	(1,784)	1,784		
		2,631		
Debt due within 1 year	(149)	149	(230)	(230)
Debt due after 1 year	(1,262)		230	(1,032)
Current asset investments	250	450		700
TOTAL	(2,903)	3,230	–	327

EXAMPLE 2   XYZ GROUP PLC
CASH FLOW STATEMENT FOR THE YEAR
ENDED 31 DECEMBER 1996

	£000	£000
Cash flow from operating		
activities (note 1)		16,022
Returns on investments and		
servicing of finance* (note 2)		(2,239)
Taxation		(2,887)
Capital expenditure and financial investment (note 2)		(865)
Acquisitions and disposals (note 2)		(17,824)
Equity dividends paid		(2,606)
Cash outflow before use of liquid resources and financing		**(10,399)**
Management of liquid resources (note 2)		700
Financing (note 2) - Issue of shares	600	
Increase in debt	2,347	
		2,947
Decrease in cash in the period		**(6,752)**

Reconciliation of net cash flow to movement in net debt (note 3)

Decrease in cash in the period	**(6,752)**	
Cash inflow from increase in debt and lease financing	(2,347)	
Cash inflow from decrease in liquid resources	(700)	
Change in net debt resulting from cash flows		(9,799)
Loans and finance leases acquired with subsidiary		(3,817)
New finance leases		(2,845)
Translation difference		643
Movement in net debt in the period		**(15,818)**
Net debt at 1.1.96		**(15,215)**
Net debt at 31.12.96		**(31,033)**

---

* *This heading would include any dividends received other than those from equity accounted entities included in operating activities.*

NOTES TO THE CASH FLOW STATEMENT

Note 1 – RECONCILIATION OF OPERATING PROFIT TO OPERATING CASH FLOWS

		Con- tinuing	Dis- continued	Total
	£000	£000	£000	£000
Operating profit		20,249	(1,616)	18,633
Depreciation charges		3,108	380	3,488
Share of profit of associate	(1,420)			
Dividend from associate	350			
Profit of associate less dividends received		(1,070)		(1,070)
Cash flow relating to previous year restructuring provision (note 4)			(560)	(560)
Increase in stocks		(11,193)	(87)	(11,280)
Increase in debtors		(3,754)	(20)	(3,774).
Increase in creditors		9,672	913	10,585
Net cash inflow from continuing operating activities		17,012		
Net cash outflow in respect of discontinued activities			(990)	
Net cash inflow from operating activities				16,022

Note 2 – ANALYSIS OF CASH FLOWS FOR HEADINGS NETTED IN THE CASH FLOW STATEMENT

	£000	£000
Returns on investments and servicing of finance		
Interest received	508	
Interest paid	(1,939)	
Preference dividend paid	(450)	
Interest element of finance lease rental payments	(358)	
Net cash outflow for returns on investments and servicing of finance		(2,239)

	£000	£000
Capital expenditure and financial investment		
Purchase of tangible fixed assets	(3,512)	
Sale of trade investment	1,595	
Sale of plant and machinery	1,052	
Net cash outflow for capital expenditure and financial investment		**(865)**
Acquisitions and disposals		
Purchase of subsidiary undertaking	(12,705)	
Net overdrafts acquired with subsidiary	(5,516)	
Sale of business	4,208	
Purchase of interest in a joint venture	(3,811)	
Net cash outflow for acquisitions and disposals		(17,824)
Management of liquid resources*		
Cash withdrawn from 7 day deposit	200	
Purchase of government securities	(5,000)	
Sale of government securities	4,300	
Sale of corporate bonds	1,200	
Net cash inflow from management of liquid resources		700
Financing		
Issue of ordinary share capital		600
Debt due within a year:		
increase in short-term borrowings	2,006	
repayment of secured loan	(850)	
Debt due beyond a year:		
new secured loan repayable in 2000	1,091	
new unsecured loan repayable in 1998	1,442	
Capital element of finance lease rental payments	(1,342)	
		2,347
Net cash inflow from financing		2,947

* XYZ Group PLC includes as liquid resources term deposits of less than a year, government securities and AA rated corporate bonds.

Note 3 - ANALYSIS OF NET DEBT

	At 1 Jan 1996	Cash Flow	Acquisition* (excl. cash and overdrafts)	Other non-cash changes	Exchange movement	At 31 Dec 1996
	£000	£000	£000	£000	£000	£000
Cash in hand, at bank	235	(1,250)			1,392	377
Overdrafts	(2,528)	(5,502)			(1,422)	(9,452)
		(6,752)				
Debt due after 1 yr	(9,640)	(2,533)	(1,749)	2,560	(792)	(12,154)
Debt due within 1 yr	(352)	(1,156)	(837)	(2,560)	1,465	(3,440)
Finance leases	(4,170)	1,342	(1,231)	(2,845)		(6,904)
		(2,347)				
Current asset investments	1,240	(700)				540
TOTAL	(15,215)	(9,799)	(3,817)	(2,845)	643	(31,033)

Note 4 - CASH FLOW RELATING TO EXCEPTIONAL ITEMS

The operating cash outflows include under discontinued activities an outflow of £560,000, which relates to the £1,600,000 exceptional provision for a fundamental restructuring made in the 1995 accounts.

* *This column would include any net debt (excluding cash and overdrafts) disposed of with a subsidiary undertaking.*

Note 5 - MAJOR NON-CASH TRANSACTIONS

a. During the year the group entered into finance lease arrangements in respect of assets with a total capital value at the inception of the leases of £2,845,000.

b. Part of the consideration for the purchases of subsidiary undertakings and the sale of a business that occurred during the year comprised shares and loan notes respectively. Further details of the acquisitions and the disposal are set out below.

Note 6 - PURCHASE OF SUBSIDIARY UNDERTAKINGS

	£000
Net assets acquired	
Tangible fixed assets	12,194
Investments	1
Stocks	9,384
Debtors	13,856
Taxation recoverable	1,309
Cash at bank and in hand	1,439
Creditors	(21,715)
Bank overdrafts	(6,955)
Loans and finance leases	(3,817)
Deferred taxation	(165)
Minority shareholders' interests	(9)
	5,522
Goodwill	16,702
	22,224
Satisfied by	
Shares allotted	9,519
Cash	12,705
	22,224

The subsidiary undertakings acquired during the year contributed £1,502,000 to the group's net operating cash flows, paid £1,308,000 in respect of net returns on investments and servicing of finance, paid £522,000 in respect of taxation and utilised £2,208,000 for capital expenditure.

Note 7 - SALE OF BUSINESS

	£000
Net assets disposed of	
Fixed assets	775
Stocks	5,386
Debtors	474
	6,635
Loss on disposal	(1,227)
	5,408
Satisfied by	
Loan notes	1,200
Cash	4,208
	5,408

The business sold during the year contributed £200,000 to the group's net operating cash flows, paid £252,000 in respect of net returns on investments and servicing of finance, paid £145,000 in respect of taxation and utilised £209,000 for capital expenditure.

EXAMPLE 3   XYZ INTERNATIONAL BANK PLC CASH FLOW STATEMENT FOR THE YEAR ENDED 31 DECEMBER 1996

Reconciliation of operating profit to net operating cash flows

	£m	£m
Operating profits		241.4
Increase in accrued income and prepayments		(161.2)
Increase in accruals and deferred income		118.1
Provision for bad and doubtful debts		20.8
Loans and advances written off net of recoveries		(50.7)
Depreciation and amortisation		42.4
Interest on subordinated loan added back		9.9
Profits on sale of investment debt and equity securities		(1.1)
Provisions for liabilities and charges		3.4
Associated undertakings - profit included	(17.8)	
dividends received	10.3	
		(7.5)
Other non-cash movements		6.3
Net cash flow from trading activities		221.8
Net increase in collections/transmissions	(81.1)	
Net increase in loans and advances to banks and customers	(1,419.1)	
Net increase in deposits by banks and customer accounts	2,542.8	
Net increase in debt securities in issue	39.9	
Net increase in non-investment debt and equity securities	(197.3)	
Net increase in other assets	(18.7)	
Net increase in other liabilities	18.6	
		885.1
Net cash inflow from operating activities		1,106.9

CASH FLOW STATEMENT

Net cash inflow from operating activities	**1,106.9**
Returns on investments and servicing of finance (note 1)	(20.5)
Taxation	(88.0)
Capital expenditure and financial investment (note 1)	(90.3)
	908.1
Acquisitions and disposals (note 1)	15.1
Equity dividends paid	(57.2)
	866.0
Financing (note 1)	6.0
Increase in cash	**872.0**

NOTES TO THE CASH FLOW STATEMENT

Note 1 - GROSS CASH FLOWS

	£m	£m
Returns on investments and servicing of finance		
Interest paid on loan capital	(9.9)	
Preference dividends paid	(10.4)	
Dividends paid to minority shareholders in subsidiary undertaking	(0.2)	
		(20.5)
Capital expenditure and financial investment		
Purchase of investment securities	(14.7)	
Sale and maturity of investment securities	5.7	
Purchase of tangible fixed assets	(121.4)	
Sales of tangible fixed assets	40.1	
		(90.3)
Acquisitions and disposals		
Investment in associated undertaking	(56.1)	
Sale of investment in associated undertaking	71.2	
		15.1
Financing		
Issue of ordinary share capital	18.3	
Repayments of loan capital	(12.3)	
		6.0

Note 2 - ANALYSIS OF THE BALANCES OF CASH AS SHOWN IN THE BALANCE SHEET

	At 1.1.96 £m	Cash flow £m	At 31.12.96 £m
Cash and balances at central banks	1,342.9	148.5	1491.4
Loans and advances to other banks repayable on demand	23,743.6	723.5	24,467.1
	25,086.5	872.0	25,958.5

The group is required to maintain balances with the Bank of England which, at 31 December 1996, amounted to £54.0 million (1995 - £43.3 million).

Certain subsidiary undertakings of the group are required by law to maintain reserve balances with the Federal Reserve Bank in the United States of America. Such reserve balances amounted to $30.4 million at 31 December 1996 (1995 - $28.6 million).

Note 3 - ANALYSIS OF CHANGES IN FINANCING DURING THE YEAR

	Share capital £m	Loan capital £m
Balances at 1 January 1996	435.3	1,248.1
Effect of foreign exchange differences		(115.7)
Cash inflow/(outflow) from financing	18.3	(12.3)
Other movements	(0.1)	
Balances at 31 December 1996	453.5	1,120.1

EXAMPLE 4 XYZ INSURANCE GROUP PLC CASH FLOW STATEMENT FOR THE YEAR ENDED 31 DECEMBER 1996

Profit on ordinary activities before tax

	£m	£m
Operating profit before taxation after interest		346.7
Depreciation of tangible fixed assets	31.6	
Increase in general insurance technical provisions	198.5	
Decrease in amounts owed by agents	18.1	
Profits relating to long-term business	(135.3)	
Cash received from long-term business (note 1)	74.0	
Share of profits of associates	(46.5)	
Dividends received from associates	22.1	
Loan interest expense	38.7	
		201.2
Net cash inflow from operating activities		547.9

CASH FLOW STATEMENT

Net cash inflow from general business	506.5	
Shareholders' net cash inflow from long-term business	74.0	
Other operating cash flows attributable to shareholders	(32.6)	
Net cash inflow from operating activities		**547.9**
Interest paid (note 2)		(41.9)
Taxation paid		(54.2)
Capital expenditure		(52.1)
Acquisitions and disposals (note 2)		(313.5)
Equity dividends paid		(135.3)
Financing (note 2)		424.6
		375.5

CASH FLOWS WERE INVESTED AS FOLLOWS:

Increase in cash holdings		**22.8**
Net portfolio investment		
(not including long-term business) (note 2)		
Ordinary shares (note 2)	127.2	
Fixed income securities (note 2)	27.9	
Investment properties (note 2)	197.6	
		352.7
Net investment of cash flows		**375.5**

Movement in opening and closing portfolio investments net of financing (note 3)

	£m	£m	£m
Net cash inflow for the period	**22.8**		
Cash flow			
Portfolio investments	352.7		
Increase in loans	(213.9)		
Movement arising from cash flows		161.6	
Movement in long-term business		82.8	
Acquired with subsidiary		145.1	
Changes in market values and exchange rate effects		142.6	
Total movement in portfolio investments net of financing			532.1
Portfolio investments net of financing at 1.1.96			**2,692.3**
Portfolio investments net of financing at 31.12.96			**3,224.4**

NOTES TO THE CASH FLOW STATEMENT

Note 1 - CASH FLOWS OF THE LONG-TERM BUSINESS (OPTIONAL)

	£m
Premiums received	497.3
Claims paid	(326.1)
Net portfolio investments	(66.9)
Other net cash flows	(14.4)
Net cash inflow before retention and transfers	89.9
Transferred to general fund	(74.0)
Cash retained in long-term business	15.9

Note 2 - ANALYSIS OF CASH FLOWS FOR HEADINGS NETTED IN THE CASH FLOW STATEMENT

	£m	£m
Interest paid		
Interest paid	(35.2)	
Interest element of finance lease rental payments	(6.7)	
		(41.9)
Acquisitions and disposals		
Acquisition of subsidiary	(330.4)	
Net cash acquired with subsidiary	16.9	
		(313.5)
Financing		
Issue of ordinary share capital	210.7	
Repayment of long-term loan	(232.7)	
New fixed rate loan repayable 2000	446.6	
Net cash inflow from financing		424.6
Portfolio investments		
Purchase of ordinary shares	(869.5)	
Purchase of fixed income securities	(1,325.3)	
Purchase of investment property	(197.6)	
Sale of ordinary shares	742.3	
Sale of fixed income securities	1,297.4	
Net cash outflow on portfolio investments		(352.7)

Note 3 - MOVEMENT IN CASH, PORTFOLIO INVESTMENTS AND FINANCING

	At 1 Jan 1996*	Cash Flow	Changes in long-term business	Acquired with subsidiary (excl. cash)	Changes to market value and currencies	Other changes	At 31 Dec 1996*
	£m	£m	£m	£m	£m	£m	£m
Cash in hand, at bank	15.3	22.8	15.9		(2.3)		51.7
Ordinary shares	1,258.1	127.2	25.1	128.4	77.2		1,616.0
Fixed income securities	2,246.7	27.9	41.8	122.8	36.4		2,475.6
Investment properties	390.5	197.6			(12.4)		575.7
		352.7					
Loans due within 1 year	(325.7)	232.7		(19.7)	16.1	(31.2)	(127.8)
Loans due after 1 year	(892.6)	(446.6)		(86.4)	27.6	31.2	(1,366.8)
		(213.9)					
TOTAL	2,692.3	161.6	82.8	145.1	142.6	–	3,224.4

* These amounts are the same as the balance sheet amounts reported by the insurance group and include amounts relating to long-term business which are required by the EC Insurance Accounts Directive to be consolidated.

Note 4 - PURCHASE OF SUBSIDIARY UNDERTAKING

	£m	£m
Net cash acquired with subsidiary undertaking	16.9	
Portfolio investments less financing acquired with subsidiary undertaking	145.1	
Other net assets	108.1	
		270.1
Goodwill		60.3
		330.4
Settled by:		
Payment of cash		330.4

The subsidiary undertaking acquired during the year contributed £57.4m to the group's net operating cash flows, paid £6.2m in respect of interest, paid £4.9m in respect of taxation and utilised £13.2m for capital expenditure.

APPENDIX II

COMPLIANCE WITH INTERNATIONAL ACCOUNTING STANDARDS

1   The International Accounting Standard on cash flows is IAS 7 'Cash Flow Statements'. IAS 7 requires an entity to present its cash flows from operating, investing and financing activities. The cash flows to be reported are inflows and outflows of cash and cash equivalents leading to the reporting of the change in cash and cash equivalents for the period. For the reasons set out in Appendix III the FRS has modified the original FRS 1, which required a cash flow statement similar to that prepared under IAS 7.

The main difference between the standards

2   The FRS defines cash flows to include only movements in cash (cash in hand and deposits repayable on demand, less overdrafts). IAS 7 defines cash flows as movements in both cash and cash equivalents. Cash equivalents are defined as short-term, highly liquid investments that are readily convertible to known amounts of cash and subject to insignificant risk of changes in value. In the FRS cash flows relating to cash equivalents are to be included in the new 'management of liquid resources' section. The narrower definition of cash in the FRS is consistent with the definition of 'cash' in IAS 7.

Minor differences between the standards

3   The requirements of the FRS also differ from IAS 7 in the following ways:

   •   IAS 7 does not have any exemptions from its scope. The FRS gives exemption to small entities, subsidiary undertakings 90 per cent of whose voting rights are controlled within the group, mutual life assurance companies, pension funds and certain open-ended investment funds. Building societies that prepare a

171

statement of source and application of funds in the prescribed format are permitted two years' exemption from the effective date of the FRS.

- IAS 7 (paragraph 22) allows the following cash flows to be reported net:

  (a) cash receipts and payments on behalf of customers when the cash flows reflect the activities of the customer rather than those of the entity; and

  (b) cash receipts and payments for items in which the turnover is quick, the amounts are large, and the maturities are short.

  Cash flows fulfilling the conditions for net reporting in paragraph 9 of the FRS would also fulfil the conditions in paragraph 22(b) of IAS 7. The FRS has no equivalent permission for cash flows relating to customers to be shown net, since for some businesses the cash flows relating to customers can be an important source of finance.

- IAS 7 classifies cash flows under three headings: 'cash flows from operating activities', 'cash flows from investing activities', and 'cash flows from financing activities'. The FRS specifies a fuller analysis using eight headings.

- Unlike the FRS, IAS 7 does not require a reconciliation of the movement in cash flows to the movement in net debt.

- IAS 7 requires cash flows of a foreign subsidiary to be translated at the exchange rates prevailing at the dates of the cash flows. A weighted average exchange rate may be used that approximates to the actual rate. The FRS states that cash flows should be translated at the same rate as the profit and loss account but allows the use of actual rates or an approximation thereto for intragroup transactions.

APPENDIX III -

THE DEVELOPMENT OF THE FRS

History

1   In September 1991 the Board issued FRS 1 'Cash Flow Statements' to replace SSAP 10 'Statements of source and application of funds'. The requirement for a cash flow statement instead of a statement of source and application of funds represented a radical change in financial reporting. In March 1994, when companies had had two years' practical experience with FRS 1, the Board called for comment on the functioning of the standard. The revised FRS is based on the subsequent proposals in FRED 10 'Revision of FRS 1 "Cash Flow Statements"' and the comments received on them.

The function of a cash flow statement

2   A cash flow statement has increasingly come to be recognised as a useful addition to the balance sheet and profit and loss account in their portrayal of financial position, performance and financial adaptability. Historical cash flow information gives an indication of the relationship between profitability and cash-generating ability, and thus of the quality of the profit earned. In addition, analysts and other users of financial information often, formally or informally, develop models to assess and compare the present value of the future cash flows of entities. Historical cash flow information could be useful to check the accuracy of past assessments and indicate the relationship between the entity's activities and its receipts and payments.

3   Assessing the opportunities and risks of an entity's business and the stewardship of its management requires an understanding of the nature of its business, which includes the way it generates and uses cash. A cash flow statement in conjunction with a profit and loss account and balance sheet provides information on financial position and performance as well as liquidity, solvency and financial adaptability. It is, therefore, important that the cash flow statement should cross-refer to the information given in the other primary statements. For this reason FRS I required a reconciliation of operating profit to cash flow from operating activities and some reconciliation with balance sheet figures. The revised FRS clarifies the link between cash flows and balance sheet movements by requiring a reconciliation between the cash flow statement and components of 'net debt', a widely used tool of financial analysis.

4   Although a cash flow statement shows information about the reporting entity's cash flows in the reporting period, it provides incomplete information for assessing future cash flows. Some cash flows result from transactions that took place in an earlier period and some cash flows are expected to result in further cash flows in a future period. Accordingly, cash flow statements should normally be used in conjunction with profit and loss accounts and balance sheets when making an assessment of future cash flows.

5   The Board specified a cash flow statement in FRS I rather than continue with a funds flow statement, which was usually based on changes in working capital, for the reasons given below.

   (a) Funds flow data based on movements in working capital can obscure movements relevant to the liquidity and solvency of an entity. For example, a significant decrease in cash available may be masked by an increase in stock or debtors. Entities may, therefore, run out of cash while reporting increases in working capital. Similarly, a decrease in working capital does not necessarily indicate a cash shortage and a danger of failure.

(b) As cash flow monitoring is a normal feature of business life and not a specialised accounting technique, cash flow is a concept that is more widely understood than are changes in working capital.

(c) Cash flows can be a direct input into a business valuation model and, therefore, historical cash flows may be relevant in a way not possible for funds flow data.

(d) A funds flow statement is based largely on the difference between two balance sheets. It reorganises such data, but does not provide new data. The cash flow statement and associated notes required by the FRS may include data not disclosed in a funds flow statement.

Changes implemented by the revised FRS

General comments

6 The comments received on the functioning of FRS 1 indicated widespread support for a cash flow statement but also a belief that the statements produced by applying FRS 1 fell short in a number of respects from what could be achieved. The Board concluded that FRS 1 could be improved to make the cash flow statement a better means of communication between preparers and users of financial statements. FRED 10's proposals for amending the cash flow standard were generally well received by the commentators and have largely been taken up in the revised FRS.

Definition of cash flows and introduction of 'management of liquid resources' section

7   The issue most often raised in the comments on FRS I was its definition of cash equivalents, although there was no · consensus on an alternative. The definition was criticised as not reflecting the way in which businesses were managed: in particular, the requirement that to be a cash equivalent an investment had to be within three months of maturity when acquired was considered unrealistic. The definition of cash equivalents had also been a controversial issue in the comments on ED 54, the exposure draft preceding FRS I. As a result of these comments the Board proposed to omit cash equivalents from cash flows and use only cash (cash in hand and deposits repayable on demand, less overdrafts) as the basis of the cash flows reported in a cash flow statement. The proposal received widespread support and the revised FRS is based on a similar definition of cash.

8   To reflect better the way that entities manage their cash and similar assets and to distinguish cash flows in relation to this activity from other investment decisions, the revised FRS has a section dealing separately with the cash flows arising from the management of liquid resources. Liquid resources are to be identified by each reporting entity according to its policy (which should be disclosed) with the proviso that they include only current asset investments. Cash flows relating to items such as short-term deposits and other cash equivalents under the original standard are to be reported as cash flows under 'management of liquid resources'. The comments supported the FRED's proposal to introduce a section for cash flows relating to the management of liquid resources.

9   The adoption of a strict cash approach and introduction of the section for cash flows relating to the management of liquid resources have the following advantages. The approach:

(a) avoids an arbitrary cut-off point in the definition of cash equivalents;

(b) distinguishes cash flows arising from accumulating or using liquid resources from those for other investing activities; and

(c) provides information about an entity's treasury activities that was not previously available to the extent that the instruments dealt in fell within the definition of cash equivalents.

Information about liquidity

10 The FRS sets out in its objective the twin purposes of a cash flow statement: to report the cash generation and cash absorption of an entity; and to provide information to assist users to assess its liquidity, solvency and financial adaptability. The majority of those commenting on FRED 10 accepted this objective but a minority believed that a cash flow statement cannot reflect appropriately changes in an entity's liquidity because it focuses only on changes in an entity's cash. Those expressing this concern usually supported a change in focus to the movement in an entity's net debt or net funds.

11 The FRS retains the focus on cash rather than using a broader measure such as net debt because the focus on cash:

•   highlights the significant components of cash that make up a cash flow statement;

- shows as cash flow movements transactions that would not be captured by a broader measure such as net debt in any case where the transaction involved an exchange of items that both fell within that broader measure;

- facilitates comparison of the cash flow performances of different entities; and

- is in line with the international focus on cash.

Recognising that movements in net debt can also provide information on an entity's liquidity, solvency and financial adaptability and are often used in discussions of performance, the revised FRS requires an analysis of the movement in net debt or net funds in the period to be given adjoining the cash flow statement or as a note to it.

Scope

12   In developing the FRS the Board has considered the comments on the scope of FRS 1 and FRED 10. Almost one-third of those commenting on FRS 1 mentioned aspects of its scope.

(a)   Small entities
At the date of issuing the revised FRS the Board has in hand a separate project reviewing the application of accounting standards to small entities. It will decide in the course of that project whether to continue the exemption of small companies from the requirement to provide a cash flow statement.

(b)   Subsidiary undertakings
The FRS exempts wholly-owned subsidiary undertakings and those where 90 per cent of the voting rights in the subsidiary undertaking are controlled within its group.

Where the parent group holds 90 per cent of the voting rights in a subsidiary undertaking it is likely that the liquidity, solvency and financial adaptability of the subsidiary undertaking will essentially depend on the group rather than its own cash flows. The exemption is conditional on consolidated financial statements in which the subsidiary undertaking is included being publicly available. The original standard exempted wholly-owned subsidiary undertakings from the requirement to provide a cash flow statement subject to a number of further conditions and the extension and simplification of the exemption was generally supported when proposed by the FRED.

(c) Pension funds

The FRS makes it clear that pension funds are exempt from preparing a cash flow statement because such a statement would add little to the information already available from the fund account and net assets statement.

(d) Investment funds

The FRS exempts open-ended investment funds from preparing a cash flow statement if three conditions are fulfilled, relating to the liquidity of investments held, whether they are held at market value and whether a statement of changes in net assets is provided. Where these conditions are met a cash flow statement for an open-ended investment fund would be of very limited additional use. Investment funds are defined in paragraph 2 of the FRS using three of the conditions for qualifying as an investment company in companies legislation. A fourth condition in the legislation requires that capital profits should not be distributed. The Board agreed with those who commented that this condition was not relevant to the exemption and that its inclusion in the standard would have unreasonably excluded unauthorised investment companies that complied with all the relevant conditions.

Format of cash flow statement

13 The Board believes that, to achieve the objectives of cash flow reporting by presenting the information in a way that is useful and easy to understand, individual cash flows should be classified according to the activity that gave rise to them. To promote comparability amongst different entities, the FRS prescribes the following standard headings: 'operating activities', 'returns on investments and servicing of finance', 'taxation', 'capital expenditure and financial investment', 'acquisitions and disposals', 'equity dividends paid', 'management of liquid resources' and 'financing'. In general the commentators supported proposals in FRED 10 to split 'investing activities' into 'capital expenditure' and 'acquisitions and disposals' and reporting dividends paid after these (in the FRS only equity dividends are included below acquisitions and disposals because the Board accepted the arguments of some commentators that non-equity dividends should be reported alongside interest paid). Except for insurance companies, the examples use a format that results in a residual amount of the increase or decrease in cash during the period. This format was preferred by those consulted on this issue, although they did not want the presentation to be mandatory. The FRS therefore follows FRED 10 in allowing reporting entities to choose the format of their cash flow statements, provided these comply with the requirements for classification and order.

14 Both in the consultation on the original cash flow standard and in that on the proposals in FRED 10 some commentators requested that the format of the cash flow statement should be changed to highlight the free cash flows of an entity. There were several interpretations of the exact composition of 'free cash flows'—indeed the commentators themselves suggested several different definitions—but a key issue was to distinguish cash flows

for investing to maintain the business from cash flows for investing to expand the business. The Board believes that it is not feasible for an accounting standard to set out how to distinguish expenditure for expansion from expenditure for maintenance. As proposed in FRED 10, the FRS requires cash flows to be analysed into those relating to capital expenditure and those relating to acquisitions and disposals. This distinction should not be interpreted as reflecting on the one hand maintenance expenditure and on the other expenditure for expansion because, depending on the circumstances, these may be included under either heading.

Gross or net cash flows

15 To allow preparers flexibility to emphasise the relevant information for their entities as they wish, the FRS allows the gross cash flows to be shown either in the cash flow statement or in a note. The FRS also allows net reporting for cash flows relating to the management of liquid resources and financing:

(a) where there is in substance a single financing transaction that fulfils the conditions in paragraph 35 of FRS 4 'Capital Instruments' (determining when committed facilities can be taken into account in determining the maturity of debt); or

(b) where the inflows and outflows are due to short maturities and high turnover occurring from rollover or reissue.

Condition (b) would allow the netting of inflows and outflows relating to a constantly renewed short-term facility or a commercial paper programme.

16 Several commentators on the original cash flow standard were concerned about whether gross presentation was appropriate for all cash flows because the volume of some investing or financing transactions was so large that their disproportionate size tended to swamp the other cash flows reported. Other commentators noted that the costs of collecting information on gross cash flows could be high while they doubted the value of that information. FRED 10 proposed that the gross amounts should be shown, in a note if preferred, for all cash flows (other than operating cash flows under the indirect method). A minority of those commenting on FRED 10 also raised concerns with the requirement for gross cash flows even in the notes. However, the Board consulted users, who confirmed that they valued the disclosure of gross amounts. The requirement for gross cash flows therefore is retained in the FRS, except that only net amounts need be shown in relation to rollover and reissue transactions. The international standard allows cash flows to be shown net where turnover is quick, amounts large and maturities short.

Classification of cash flows

17 The FRS requires that a cash flow should be classified according to the substance of the transaction or event that gave rise to it. The substance of a transaction may be determined by applying an accounting standard (for example, SSAP 21 'Accounting for leases and hire purchase contracts', FRS 4 'Capital Instruments' or FRS 5 'Reporting the Substance of Transactions'). The approach based on substance should result in transactions and events being treated on the same basis in cash flow statements as in the other primary statements where treatment is also determined by substance. However, to give a complete picture of interest cash flows in a period, the FRS requires all interest cash flows to be reported under servicing of finance, even if some interest is capitalised in the other financial statements.

Direct or indirect cash flows

18 In developing FRS 1 the Board considered the respective merits of the so-called 'direct' and 'indirect' methods for reporting net cash flow from operating activities. The principal advantage of the direct method is that it shows operating cash receipts and payments. Knowledge of the specific sources of cash receipts and the purposes for which cash payments were made in past periods may be useful in assessing future cash flows. However, the Board noted that it did not believe that in all cases the benefits to users of this information outweighed the costs to the reporting entity of providing it and, therefore, did not require the information to be given. The Board remains of this view, and the FRS continues to encourage the direct method only where the potential benefits to users outweigh the costs of providing it.

Reconciliation of operating profit to operating cash flows

19 The FRS permits the reconciliation of operating profit to operating cash flows to be shown either adjoining the cash flow statement, if it is separately identified and clearly labelled, or as a note. Although many commentators welcomed the proposal in FRED 10 to allow the reconciliation to appear above the cash flow statement, others believed the effect would be to detract from the emphasis on cash flows by wedging the statement itself between two reconciliations—one to operating profit, the other to net debt—neither of which represented cash flows. While not prohibiting such a presentation, the wording in the FRS would also permit both reconciliations to follow the primary statement. Some commentators were concerned about how cash flows in relation to provisions should be classified in cash flow statements. The FRS makes it clear that cash flows from operating activities should include cash flows in respect of operating items in relation to any provision, whether on acquisitions, or on termination or for a fundamental reorganisation or restructuring (under paragraph 20a and b of FRS 3).

Dividends from equity accounted entities should also be included as cash flows from operating activities if the results of those entities are included in operating profit.

Banks

20 The Board has discussed the application of the requirement for a cash flow statement with representatives of the banking industry. The banks had argued for exemption during the development of FRS 1 on the basis that a bank's cash is its stock-in-trade and that more useful information would be given by a statement dealing with the capital resources available to the bank. The Board agreed that capital resources were an important indicator of the solvency and financial adaptability of financial institutions, but also believed that a cash flow statement could provide users of financial statements published by banks with useful information on the sources of cash and how it had been utilised. The Board remains of the view that cash flow statements for banks contain information on their generation and use of cash that may be useful to the users of their financial statements, and the FRS contains no exemption for banks.

21 Example 3 in Appendix I shows a cash flow statement for a bank. The special nature of banking and its regulation is recognised in the format headings and by splitting the cash flows from operating activities to show separately the cash flows from trading. A bank may hold a wide range of investments of different maturities for trading or investment and manage its liquidity in relation to all its assets and liabilities. It is therefore difficult to make a meaningful distinction by attempting to identify cash flows that relate to the management of a bank's liquid resources. Banking entities are not required to provide a reconciliation to net debt because, given the nature of their business, changes in net debt have limited meaning. Other measures, such as regulatory capital ratios, may give a better appreciation of a bank's solvency and financial adaptability.

Building societies

22 FRED 10 proposed that building societies should prepare cash flow statements on the same basis as banks and that their existing exemption should be ended. The proposal depended on changes in the legislation on financial reporting by building societies to make it effective. The Board still believes that the proposals in FRED 10 were correct, given the similarity and competition between the banks and building societies. However, the FRS has extended the existing exemption for building societies for a further two years to develop a consensus on cash flow statements and related aspects of financial reporting for banks and building societies.

Insurance companies and groups

23 In developing the FRS the Board considered the application of FRS 1 to insurance companies and groups. Comments from the insurance industry had raised several issues that were believed to arise because of the special nature of the business. A general issue raised was the meaning of a cash flow statement for an insurance company. The special implications of cash flow statements for insurance companies are discussed in paragraph 62 of the Explanation. The FRS encourages segmentation of the cash flows to assist users to understand the nature of the reporting entity's cash flows and the relationship between them. One suggestion is to use segmentation to reflect different degrees of access to cash balances. This would allow insurance companies to divide their businesses into segments to reflect the degree of access that shareholders had to cash balances.

24 The Board believes that cash flows arising from the long-term business of an insurance company or group should be dealt with in the cash flow statement only to the extent of cash transferred to, and available to meet the obligations of, the company or group as a whole. The internal cash flows of the long-term business may be shown in a note to the cash flow statement. The Board takes this approach because the shareholders of an insurance company generally have restricted rights to any profits, and associated cash surpluses, made by the long-term business. Because insurance companies and groups are now required by companies legislation to consolidate the long-term business, these funds need to be included in the note to the cash flow statement analysing the changes in the balance sheet amounts for portfolio investments net of financing.

25 Appendix I contains an example of a cash flow statement for an insurance group. By including a section showing the cash flows relating to portfolio investments, this format recognises the special nature of an insurance business, in particular the importance of generating resources for investment to meet provision requirements for future claims and reserve requirements for solvency. The example for insurance companies contains an analysis of the movement in portfolio investments less financing rather than an analysis of net debt as generally required. Presenting information on portfolio investments less financing recognises that the required balance sheet format for insurance companies does not distinguish between fixed and current financial assets.

Exceptional and extraordinary items and cash flows

26 To reflect the changes introduced by FRS 3 'Reporting Financial Performance', the text now acknowledges the extreme rarity of extraordinary items post-FRS 3. The FRS also explicitly recognises the possibility that cash flows can be exceptional of themselves because of their size or incidence without relating to an exceptional item in the profit and loss account. Sufficient disclosure should be made to explain their cause and nature.

Value Added Tax and other taxes

27 The existence of Value Added Tax (VAT), and other sales taxes, raises the question whether the relevant cash flows should be reported gross or net of the tax element and how the balance of tax paid to, or repaid by, the taxing authorities should be reported. Generally, sales taxes, including VAT, are payable by the ultimate consumer of the goods or services concerned. A business providing goods or services on which VAT is payable (even if at a zero rate) is generally able to reclaim the VAT incurred by it in providing those goods or services. However, businesses that make exempt supplies are unable to reclaim VAT. Between these two categories are partially exempt businesses that can reclaim part of the VAT incurred by them.

28 The cash flows of an entity include VAT where appropriate and thus strictly the various elements of the cash flow statement should include VAT. However, this treatment does not take into account the fact that normally VAT is a short-term timing difference as far as the entity's overall cash flows are concerned and the inclusion of VAT in the cash flows may distort the allocation of cash flows to standard headings. In order to avoid this distortion and to show cash flows attributable to the reporting entity's activities, the Board believes that cash flows should be shown net of sales taxes and the net movement on the amount payable to, or receivable from, the taxing authority should be allocated to cash flows from operating activities unless a different treatment is more appropriate in the particular circumstances concerned.

Foreign exchange

29 To meet the concern that intragroup cash inflows and outflows might not cancel each other out if average or closing rates are used to translate them for preparing consolidated cash flow statements, the FRS permits entities to use actual rates for intragroup cash flows envisaging that these will be applied where there are large single cash flows at rates significantly different from the average or closing rate used for the other cash flows. Several commentators had raised the treatment of foreign currency in cash flow statements. Because of the various approximations that may be required in particular cases, the Board has not sought to specify in detail the methods to be used to deal with foreign exchange differences. It has, however, set out the principle that in translating the cash flows of foreign entities the same basis should be used as for the translation of the profit and loss account. The FRS now clarifies that this principle applies also to the presentation of stocks, debtors and creditors in the reconciliation from operating profits and cash flow from operating activities.

Hedging

30 FRS 1 required cash flows that result from transactions undertaken to hedge another transaction to be reported under the same standard heading as the transaction that is the subject of the hedge. Several commentators expressed concern that the FRS 1 requirement relating to hedging was too broad, for example it could justify cash flows relating to loans taken out to finance overseas investment being classified under 'investing' rather than 'financing'. To meet these concerns the FRS requires that the effect of hedging should be reflected in the cash flow statement only where hedging is by futures contracts, forward contracts, option contracts or swap contracts. This is a pragmatic position that follows the US cash flow standard while awaiting the outcome of the Board's project on derivatives and other financial instruments, which will consider all aspects of hedging and its recognition.

FRS 3 'Reporting Financial Performance'

31   The FRS encourages entities to analyse cash flows on the same basis as that required by FRS 3 in the profit and loss account and to show separately cash flows relating to continuing and discontinued operations. There was widespread support for such analyses when proposed by FRED 10 but commentators did not support a requirement for them.

Restrictions on remittability

32   Several of the comments received on FRS 1 had indicated that disclosures of restricted cash balances would be useful. FRED 10 proposed the disclosure of cash not available for use elsewhere in the group. The FRS requires disclosure for both businesses and groups of the circumstances and effect of restrictions preventing the transfer of cash from one part to another. Paragraph 68 of the Explanation gives examples of items that, depending on the regulatory environment, might be required to be disclosed.

Checklist to the requirements of FRS 1 (revised) 1996

1 General Requirements

1.1 *Note*: The FRS applies to all financial statements FRS 1 para 5
intended to -give a true and fair view of the financial
position and profit or loss (or income and expenditure)
except those of:

   (a) subsidiary undertakings where 90 per cent or more
of the voting rights are controlled within the group,
provided that consolidated financial statements in
which the subsidiary undertakings are included are
publicly available.

   (b) mutual life assurance companies.

   (c) pension funds.

   (d) open-ended investment funds that meet all the
following conditions:

      (i) substantially all of the entity's investments are
highly liquid;

      (ii) substantially all of the entity's investments are
carried at market value; and

      (iii) the entity provides a statement of changes in
net assets.

   (e) for two years from the effective date of the FRS,
building societies, as defined by the Building
Societies Act 1986 in the UK and by the Building
Societies Act 1989 in the Republic of Ireland, that
prepare, as required by law, a statement of source
and application of funds in a prescribed format.

   (f) companies incorporated under companies legislation
and entitled to exemptions available in the
legislation for small companies when filing accounts
with the Registrar of Companies.

   (g) entities that would have been in category (f) above
if they were companies incorporated under
companies legislation.

1.2	Where an entity is required to prepare a cash flow statement, do the financial statements include a cash flow statement as a primary statement?	FRS 1 para 4
1.3	Does the statement include all the reporting entity's inflows and outflows of cash, and exclude transactions that do not result in cash flows of the reporting entity ?	FRS 1 para 6

1.4 Does the statement list the entity's cash flows for the   FRS 1 para 7
period classified under the following headings:
- operating activities?
- returns on investments and servicing of finance?
- taxation?
- capital expenditure and financial investment?
- acquisitions and disposals?
- equity dividends paid?
- management of liquid resources?
- financing?

1.5 Are the first six headings given in the sequence set out   FRS 1 para 7
above?

1.6 Are the cash flows and subtotals for each of   FRS 1 para 7
'management of liquid resources' and 'financing' shown
separately, where they have been combined under a
single heading in the cash flow statement?

1.7 Are the individual categories of inflows and outflows   FRS 1 para 8
under the standard headings disclosed separately (except
where permitted to be shown net, see below), where
material, in the cash flow statement or in a note?
Note: Cash flows relating to operating activities may be   FRS 1 para 9
shown net. Cash inflows and outflows within the
management of liquid resources or financing may also be
netted against each other if they either:
- (a) relate in substance to a single financing transaction (which is one that fulfils the conditions in paragraph 35 of FRS 4 'Capital Instruments'); or
- (b) are due to short maturities and high turnover occurring from rollover or reissue (for example, short-term deposits or a commercial paper programme).

2   Operating activities

2.1   Does the net cash flow from operating activities represent FRS 1 para 11
the net movement in cash resulting from operations
shown in the profit and loss account in arriving at
operating profit?

2.2   Does the net cash flow from operating activities include   FRS 1 para 11
cash flows in respect of operating items relating to
provisions, whether or not the provision was included in
operating profit?

2.3   Does the net cash flow from operating activities include   FRS 1 para 11
dividends received from equity accounted entities where
the results are included as part of operating profit?

2.4   Is a reconciliation between operating profit and the net   FRS 1 para 12
cash flow from operating activities given either adjoining
the cash flow statement or as a note?

Note: (a) If adjoining the cash flow statement, it should
be clearly labelled and kept separate.
(b) This reconciliation should disclose separately
the movements in stock, debtors and creditors
related to operating activities and other differences
between cash flows and profits.
(c) This reconciliation should also show separately
the difference between dividends received and
results taken into account for equity accounted
entities.

3   Returns on investments and servicing of finance

3.1   Are the following categories of cash inflows and
outflows shown separately under the standard heading
'returns on investments and servicing of finance':

- interest received, including any related tax   FRS 1 para 14(a)
recovered?

- dividends received, net of any tax credits (except   FRS 1 para 14(b)
dividends from equity accounted entities whose
results are included as part of operating profit)?

- interest paid (even if capitalised), including any tax   FRS 1 para 15(a)
deducted and paid to the relevant tax authority?

- cash flows that are treated as finance costs under   FRS 1 para 15(b)
FRS 4 (this will include issue costs on debt and
non-equity share capital)?

- the interest element of finance lease rental payments?   FRS 1 para 15(c)
- dividends paid on non-equity shares of the entity?   FRS 1 para 15(d)
- dividends paid to minority interests?   FRS 1 para 15(e)

4   Taxation

4.1   Do cash flows included under the heading 'taxation' only   FRS 1 para 16
relate to cash flows in respect of taxation arising from
revenue and capital profits?

Note: Cash flows in respect of other taxation, including   FRS 1 para 16
payments and receipts in respect of Value Added Tax,
other sales taxes, property taxes and other taxes not
assessed on the profits of the reporting entity, should be
dealt with as set out in section 14.

4.2   For a subsidiary undertaking, do cash flows included   FRS 1 para 16
under the heading 'taxation' include cash flows relating
to group relief?

4.3   Do the taxation cash flows in 4.1 above include:

- cash receipts from the relevant tax authority of tax   FRS 1 para 17
  rebates, claims or returns of overpayments ?
- cash payments to the relevant tax authority of tax,   FRS 1 para 18
  including payments of advance corporation tax?

4.4   Do the taxation cash flows in 4.2 above include:

- payments received from other members of the   FRS 1 para 17
  group for group relief?
- payments made to other members of the group for   FRS 1 para 18
  group relief?

5   Capital expenditure and financial investment

5.1   Do cash flows included under the heading 'capital   FRS 1 para 19
expenditure and financial investment' only relate to the
acquisition or disposal of any fixed asset other than one
required to be classified under 'acquisitions and
disposals' as specified in section 6, and any current asset
investment not included in liquid resources as specified
in section 8?

Note: If no cash flows relating to financial investment   FRS 1 para 19
fall to be included under this heading, the caption maybe
reduced to 'capital expenditure'

5.2　Are the following categories of cash flows included
under the heading 'capital expenditure and financial
investment':

- receipts from sales or disposals of property, plant　　FRS 1 para 20(a)
  or equipment?
- receipts from the repayment of the reporting　　　　FRS 1para 20(b)
  entity's loans to other entities or sales of debt
  instruments of other entities other than receipts
  forming part of an acquisition or disposal or a
  movement in liquid resources, as specified
  respectively in sections 6 and 8?
- payments to acquire property, plant or equipment?　FRS 1para 21(a)

- loans made by the reporting entity and payments to　FRS 1para 21(b)
  acquire debt instruments of other entities other than
  payments forming part of an acquisition or disposal
  or a movement in liquid resources, as specified
  respectively in sections 6 and 8?

6　Acquisitions and disposals

6.1　Do cash flows included under the heading 'acquisitions　FRS 1 para 22
and disposals' only relate to the acquisition or disposal of
any trade or business, or of an investment in an entity
that is or, as a result of the transaction, becomes or
ceases to be either an associate, a joint venture, or a
subsidiary undertaking?

6.2　Are the following categories of cash flows included
under the heading 'acquisitions and disposals':

- receipts from sales of investments in subsidiary　　FRS 1 para 23(a)
  undertakings, showing separately any balances of
  cash and overdrafts transferred as part of the sale?
- receipts from sales of investments in associates or　FRS 1 para 23(b)
  joint ventures?
- receipts from sales of trades or businesses?　　　　FRS 1 para 23(c)
- payments to acquire investments in subsidiary　　　FRS 1 para 24(a)
  undertakings, showing separately any balances of
  cash and overdrafts acquired?
- payments to acquire investments in associates and　FRS 1 para 24(b)
  joint ventures?
- payments to acquire trades or businesses?　　　　　FRS 1 para 24(c)

7 Equity dividends paid

7.1 Do the cash flows included in 'equity dividends paid'   FRS 1 para 25
only relate to dividends paid on the reporting entity's, or,
in a group, the parent's, equity shares, excluding any
advance corporation tax?

8 Management of liquid resources

8.1 Does "management of liquid resources' include cash   FRS 1 para 26
flows in respect of current asset investments held as
readily disposable stores of value?
Note: A readily disposable investment is one that: FRS 1 para 2
(a)   is disposable by the reporting entity without
curtailing or disrupting its business: and is either:
(b)(i)   readily convertible into known amounts of cash at
or close to its carrying amount, or
(b)(ii)   traded in an active market.

8.2 Does the reporting entity explain what it includes as   FRS 1 para 26
liquid resources and any changes in its policy?

8.3 Are the following cash flows included under
'management of liquid resources':
- withdrawals from short-term deposits not   FRS 1 para 27(a)
qualifying as cash in so far as not netted under
section 1.7?
- inflows from disposal or redemption of any other   FRS 1 para 27(b)
investments held as liquid resources?
- payments into short-term deposits not qualifying   FRS 1 para 28(a)
as cash in so far as not netted under section 1.7?
- outflows to acquire any other investments held as   FRS 1 para 28(b)
liquid resources?

9 Financing

9.1 Are the following categories of cash flows shown
separately under 'financing':
- receipts from issuing shares or other equity   FRS 1 para 30(a)
instruments?
- receipts from issuing debentures, loans, notes, and   FRS 1 para 30(b)
bonds and from other long-term and short-term
borrowings (other than overdrafts)?

■	repayments of amounts borrowed (other than overdrafts)?	FRS 1 para 31(a)
■	the capital element of finance lease rental payments?	FRS 1 para 31(b)
■	payments to reacquire or redeem the entity's shares?	FRS 1 para 31(c)
■	payments of expenses or commissions on any issue of equity shares?	FRS 1 para 31(d)

10 Reconciliation to net debt

10.1 Is a reconciliation between the movement of cash in the   FRS 1 para 33
period and the movement in net debt given either
adjoining the cash flow statement or in a note?
Note: if adjoining the cash flow statement, it should be
clearly labelled and kept separate.

10.2 Are the changes in net debt analysed from the opening to   FRS 1 para 33
the closing component amounts showing separately,
where material, changes resulting from:
(a)   the cash flows of the entity;
(b)   the acquisition or disposal of subsidiary
         undertakings;
(c)   other non-cash changes; and
(d)   the recognition of changes in market value and
         exchange rate movements.?
Note: Where several balance sheet amounts or part   FRS 1 para 33
thereof have to be combined to form the components of
opening and closing net debt, sufficient detail should be
shown to enable the cash and other components of net
debt to be respectively traced back to the amounts shown
under the equivalent captions in the balance sheet.

11 Exceptional and extraordinary items and cash flows

11.1 In respect of cash flows that are classified as exceptional
or extraordinary items in the profit and loss account, are
the cash flows dealt with in the following ways:
■   classified under the appropriate standard headings FRS 1 para 37
         according to the nature of each item?

- identified in the cash flow statement or a note to   FRS 1 para 37
it and the relationship between the cash flows and
the originating exceptional or extraordinary item
explained?

11.2 In respect of cash flows that are exceptional because of   FRS 1 para 38
their size or incidence but are not related to items that
are treated as exceptional or extraordinary in the profit
and loss account, are the cash flows disclosed in
sufficient detail to explain their cause and nature?

12   Value added tax and other taxes

12.1 In respect of VAT and other sales taxes, are the cash   FRS 1 para 39
flows dealt with in the following ways:
- by reporting cash flows net of VAT and other
sales taxes?
- by including the net movement on the amount
payable to, or receivable from, the taxing
authority in cash flows from operating activities
unless a different treatment is more appropriate in
the particular circumstances concerned?

12.2 Are cash flows reported gross of any irrecoverable VAT   FRS 1 para 39
and other sales taxes?

12.3 Where it is impracticable to show cash flows gross of the   FRS 1 para 39
irrecoverable tax, is the irrecoverable tax shown under
the most appropriate heading?

12.4 Are other taxation cash flows, excluding those relating to   FRS 1 para 40
income taxes, corporation taxes, VAT and other sales
taxes, shown under the same standard heading as the
cash flow that gave rise to them, unless a different
treatment is more appropriate in the particular
circumstances concerned?

13   Foreign currencies

13.1 Are cash flows of foreign entities translated at the same   FRS 1 para 41
rate as that used for translating the results of the foreign
entities for inclusion in the profit and loss account?

13.2 Are movements in stocks, debtors and creditors in the   FRS 1 para 41
reconciliation between operating profit and cash from
operating activities, translated at the same rate as that
used for translating the results of the foreign entities for
inclusion in the profit and loss account?

13.3 If the rate used to translate intra-group cash flows is not   FRS 1 para 41
the actual rate, have any exchange rate differences arising
been included in the effect of exchange rate movements
shown as part of the reconciliation to net debt?

14 Hedging transactions

14.1 Are cash flows arising from futures contracts, forward   FRS 1 para 42
contracts, option contracts or swap contracts accounted
for as hedges, reported under the same standard headings
as the transactions that are the subject of the hedge?

15 Consolidated financial statements

15.1 When preparing consolidated cash flow statements, are   FRS 1 para 43
adjustments made to eliminate those cash flows that are
internal to the group?

15.2 Where a group has investments in entities that are
included in the consolidation under the equity method,
are the cash flows between the group and the entities
concerned dealt with in the followings ways:

■   By including only the actual cash flows between   FRS 1 para 44
the group and the entities concerned (that is, not
the cash flows of the equity accounting entity
itself)?

■   By including dividends received from the entities
concerned in one of the following ways:

    ■ Included in operating cash flows where the   FRS 1 para 11
results of the entities concerned are included
as part of operating profit and separate
disclosure made of the difference between   FRS 1 para 12
dividends received and their results in the
reconciliation of operating profit to operating
cash flows?

■ Disclosed separately under 'returns on investments and servicing of finance' where the results of the entities concerned are included outside of operating profit?   FRS 1 para 14(a)

■ Are financing cash flows received from or paid to the entities concerned disclosed separately under 'financing'?   FRS 1 para 32

15.3 Where a group acquires or disposes of a subsidiary undertaking during the year, are the cash flows relating to the acquisition and disposal dealt with in the followings ways:

■ Are the cash flows of the subsidiary for the same period as the group's profit and loss account which includes the results of the subsidiary?   FRS 1 para 43

■ Is there a note to the statement that discloses a summary of the effects of the acquisitions and disposals, indicating how much of the consideration comprised cash?   FRS 1 para 45

■ Where material, is there a note to the statement that discloses the extent to which the amounts reported under each of the standard headings have been affected by the cash flows of the subsidiary acquired or disposed of?   FRS 1 para 45

16 Banks

16.1 Does 'banks' include as cash only cash and balances at central banks and loans and advances to banks repayable on demand?   FRS 1 para 34

16.2 Do cash flows from operating activities include: FRS 1 para 34
    ■ receipts and payments relating to loans made to other entities? and
    ■ cash flows relating to investments held for trading?

Note: A bank need not include a section on the management of liquid resources nor the reconciliation of cash flows to the movement in net debt.   FRS 1 para 34

17   Insurance companies and groups

17.1   Does the reconciliation of operating profit to net cash   FRS 1 para 35
flow from operating activities take profit or loss on
ordinary activities before tax as its starting point?

17.2   For insurance companies and groups, other than mutual   FRS 1 para 35
life assurance companies to which the FRS does not
apply, are cash flows of long-term business, long-term
life, pensions and annuity businesses or their equivalents
in relation to overseas operations, only included to the   FRS 1 para 36
extent of cash transferred and available to meet the
obligations of the company or group as a whole?

17.3   Is there a section for cash flows relating to 'portfolio   FRS 1 para 35
investments' rather than a section for cash flows relating
to the 'management of liquid resources'?

17.4   Is an analysis of the movement in portfolio investments   FRS 1 para 36
less financing provided instead of the analysis of the
movement in net debt?
Note: The note should distinguish movements relating to
the long-term business to the extent that these are
included in the balance sheet amounts.

18   Other note disclosure

18.1   Are material non-cash transactions disclosed in the notes   FRS 1 para 46
to the cash flow statement if disclosure is necessary in
order to understand the underlying transactions?

18.2   Are the amounts and circumstances where restrictions   FRS 1 para 47
prevent the transfer of cash from one part of the business
or group to another explained in the notes to the cash
flow statement?

18.3   Are comparative figures given for all items in the cash   FRS 1 para 49
flow statement and notes?
Note: Comparatives are not required for the note to the
statement that analyses changes in the balance sheet
amounts making up net debt (or the equivalent note for
insurance companies and groups) and the note of the
material effect of acquisitions and disposal of subsidiary
undertakings on each of the standard headings.

Index

(References are to page)

203